NEW MEXICO MAGAZINE'S

MORE OF THE BEST FROM
NEW MEXICO KITCHENS

BY
SHEILA MACNIVEN CAMERON
AND
THE STAFF OF NEW MEXICO MAGAZINE

NEW MEXICO MAGAZINE, SANTA FE, NM
USA

ALSO BY SHEILA MACNIVEN CAMERON
THE HIGHLANDER'S COOKBOOK
HOMEMADE ICE CREAMS AND SHERBETS
THE BEST FROM NEW MEXICO KITCHENS

LIBRARY OF CONGRESS CATALOGUE CARD
NUMBER: 82-062076
ISBN NUMBER: 0-937206-02-4
© NEW MEXICO MAGAZINE, 1983

DESIGNED BY BONNIE BISHOP TREMPER
ILLUSTRATIONS BY JOAN McCONNELL
COVER PHOTOGRAPH BY MARK NOHL

CONTENTS

INTRODUCTION

One of the nice things about New Mexico is that we're all members of minority groups. "A cultural mosaic" sounds like a clever tourist promotional phrase—but it's nonetheless true in this state where even the largest minorities are divided into a multiplicity of subgroups. The best part of this ethnic diversity is that everyone has contributed something to the culture—and especially to the kitchen.

The bedrock of New Mexico cuisine is, of course, Pueblo Indian, reaching back untold thousands of years. The basic ingredients of corn, beans, squash, chile, game, and wild fruits and vegetables were adapted and augmented by Navajo and Apache, then by the Spanish colonists who arrived here more than 300 years ago. On this Indian-Spanish foundation were laid the influences of later groups who began arriving less than 150 years ago—French, Mexicans, English, Scots, Irish, and Germans; Yankees, Midwesterners, and Southerners of every color and every persuasion. Italians, Lebanese, Scandinavians, Greeks, Chinese and more came and added their individual touches. Recent times have brought Indonesians, South Africans, South Americans, Japanese, all contributing something of their own backgrounds.

Many immigrants moved on or were absorbed into the prevalent Indian-Spanish culture, leaving behind only a breath of mysterious difference—a French village, a Yugoslavian surname, an Australian apple tree—and always, new ways of cooking things.

In *The Best from New Mexico Kitchens*, we gave you a big helping of good New Mexico cooking—from Indian-Spanish basics to haute cuisine. Now it's time for another feast. Here are different versions of classic New Mexico dishes, forgotten favorites of the pioneers and of our parents, familiar recipes with new twists. They range from supremely simple to elegantly sophisticated, from cottage casseroles to regal desserts.

Of course you won't get far with New Mexico cooking if you don't know the basics: how to cook beans, how to prepare fresh chile, how to make chile sauce and tortillas. So we've included a chapter on these, and we've scattered a few classics through the various other sections.

We have here specialities from restaurants big and small—places you may have visited yourself—and from good cooks all over the state. As is to be expected, everyone makes good use of New Mexico's agricultural products: beef, lamb, apples, pecans, peanuts, corn, squash, beans, and—what else?—chile.

Finally, just for fun, we asked a number of well-known New Mexicans to tell us their favorite recipes, and we got some surprising results. You'll find their often humorous and always tasty replies in the last chapter of this book.

We hope you enjoy our recipes, the food, and good health always. ¡Salud!

by John Crenshaw

Humble, lowly, some say of the bean; but in its blossoms flowered civilizations, from its seeds grew cities.

In ruins left by people of the San Juan region of northwestern New Mexico about 1,500 years ago, archaeologists have read signs of transition. Families in this area and in neighboring Colorado began moving out of pithouses and building larger villages of above-ground homes, forerunners to the mighty cities of Mesa Verde, Aztec, and Chaco Canyon. Setting aside their atlatls, these hunters drew bow to arrow to pierce game or enemy. Their artisans rolled clay into sinuous ropes, coiling them circle upon circle to fashion pots. These they fired in pyres of piñon, making cooking and storage vessels superior even to the excellent baskets they replaced.

Momentous changes, these, pivots upon which civilizations turn; but no less momentous as an element in change, these people planted, tended, harvested, dried, stored, soaked, cooked, and ate—beans.

While one can never discount corn's importance as a swayer of New World peoples' paths from those of hunting and gathering societies to those of town-building farmers, corn and squash had predated beans in the region by centuries without having had that effect. Beans, nourishing farm and farmer alike, completed the triad of foods that in large part supported the great Pueblo cultures and has ever since fueled the work of man in *Nuevo México*.

For centuries, it appears, early New Mexicans planted corn in likely spots and left it virtually unattended while foraging for wild plants and game, returning in autumn to harvest whatever the deer and 'coons had left. Beans took more tending, indicating the beginnings of a more settled life—perhaps even requiring it.

Too, beans added substantial new calories to the diet of those who stayed to tend them. Beans' complex carbohydrates—the starches so mismaligned by modern-day faddists—were a good balance to the simple carbohydrates of corn. Easily disgested, "healthful" complex carbohydrates feed the body a steady stream of energy. A bowl of beans powers a geologist tramping across the high deserts or a skier schussing down the slopes of Sierra Blanca just as it fueled a prehistoric mason laying his courses of stone.

A need for tending and a contribution of calories were important, but beans' proteins boosted both their own and corn's consequence— for as stones are to a mason's walls, so are proteins to the stonemason's body. Meat supplies it, but meat had to be caught by net, snare, pit, club, arrow, or darting hand. Wild animal numbers could not meet the needs of burgeoning populations, nor could corn or beans alone; but what corn lacks, beans bring. Eating the two together increases by half again the amount of complete, usable protein gained by eating them separately. They fit together as neatly as any joint or corner at Chaco Canyon's Pueblo Bonito.

Corn and beans, then, supplied two essentials of life—proteins and carbohydrates. Squash, third leg of the triangle, fed fats into the diet, not through its meat, but through its richly oiled seeds.

The trio were equally teamed in the field, coming to be planted together in little hills, where each served the other. Corn and squash could be planted at the same time, beans when the corn was a few inches high. Corn stalks thus became beanpoles; beans and corn shad- ed squash; squash spread broad leaves as a ground cover, conserv- ing water for all; beans, being legumes, fed enriching nitrogen into the soil as they grew and added still more after harvest, through decay of leaves and vines left in the field.

With food assured through crops—and supplemented most certain- ly by the vitamin-rich flavorful demigod chile and by harvest of game ranging in size from field mice, rabbits, and prairie dogs through badgers and birds to bighorn sheep, and by gathered roots, bulbs, grass and sunflower seeds, piñon nuts and acorns, berries and cac- tus fruit—there was time enough to build cities several stories high, to build commerce and government, myth and religion—to build civilizations.

Having come along at the right time, beans earned a place in history, albeit one often overlooked, and have fed New Mexicans for hundreds of years.

Indians were growing beans before the Spaniards arrived, and the Spaniards brought beans with them. Beans—typically *Phaseolus vulgaris L*, the species including the many varieties of pinto, kidney, and other common beans—were common indeed to the diet of all, continuing as part of the same triad that had successfully sustained Indians. With the addition of livestock, dairy products, fruits, and wheat from the Spaniards, everyone's diet improved further. (Wheat proteins also pair well with those of beans; the protein gain is about a third.)

No party of *ciboleros* rode to the plains without beans, cooked perhaps by an old man over a fire of buffalo chips left by the hunters' quarry. The trade caravans of ox-drawn *carretas* carried beans as provender. *El pastor*, when he moved his flock of sheep, left a pot of *frijoles* simmering in a bed of coals and ashes underground. *Peones* trudged from the fields and *vaqueros* galloped in from roundup to the same fare that their *patrón* ate off better plates.

When *los gringos* came, they ate beans. Bunkhouse cooks were never known for inventiveness; and beans, biscuits, and beef were on the board noon and night. The feller who dropped pines burned beans with each swing of his axe. The sawyer who shaped trees into crossties and mine shorings had beans for breakfast. The miner driving his pick into coal beneath the shorings, the gandy dancer driving spikes into the crossties, the engineer driving his train over the track—all drove on beans.

Storekeepers bought beans, sold beans, ate beans. Schoolboy and schoolteacher alike were filled on beans. The burro the schoolboy jigged to school even ate from the bean plant, being fed on the stalks, stems, and leaves of the plants after harvest. Homesteaders grew them, ate them, and went broke on them: the food of the Depression, beans, made survivors.

And when New Mexicans today say beans, they don't mean just any old bean. It must be the pinto—a fat, speckled oval that cooks up dusty pink. Mystified folks from other realms may know them as borlotti beans, but here we know the freckled beauties are painted, spotted, mottled—in a word, pinto.

Greek tragic plays, however, teach us of flawed heroes; and as it was with heroic Greeks, so it is with beans. Tragic heroes' sin was pride, and in some of the less memorable plays, it led to gassy speeches. In unpretentious beans no fault of hubris lies; the flaw is simply gas.

Soaking them overnight, then draining and rinsing them (some recommend up to three such long soaks) is said to remove the compounds that react in the gut with such noisy and noisome result. Maybe it works; the alternative is simply to enjoy a bowl of beans, the poor man's protein, and let its flaw pass.

FRIJOLES

One would think that a boiled bean is a boiled bean. But it's not that simple, of course. Each cook thinks his or her way is the best—and only—method.

Those who advocate the overnight soak will do it this way: Take 2 cups of dry pinto beans, pick them over, and wash them. Cover with cold water and soak overnight. Drain and rinse well. Put in a large pot with about 8 cups of water and 2 tablespoons of lard. Bring to a boil and simmer gently, covered, for about 1½ hours, then test for tenderness. Stir in 2 teaspoons of salt. Depending on how long the beans were soaked and how high your altitude is (the temperature at which things boil goes down as altitude goes up), you may have to cook the beans for up to another hour, adding more water if needed. Serve beans, broth and all, in bowls. Top with red or green chile salsa.

Most people do it this way: Pick over the 2 cups of dry pinto beans and wash them. Put beans, 8 cups of water, and 2 tablespoons of lard in a big pot. Some folks like to add 2 cloves of garlic. Bring to a boil, cover, and simmer for 2 hours, 2½ if you are at a high altitude. Stir in 2 teaspoons of salt. (If you add salt too early in the cooking, your beans will be too tough.) Continue cooking, adding water as necessary, until beans are tender. Serve as above.

Another way to cook your pinto beans is in the pressure cooker. Pick over 2 cups of dry pinto beans and wash them. Put beans, 8 cups of water and 2 tablespoons of lard into a large pressure cooker. Bring to a boil and boil gently for 10 minutes without the lid on. Remove from heat, cover, and let the beans stand for about 2 hours, or until an hour before you intend to eat. Add 2 teaspoons salt, cover and bring the pressure up to 15 pounds. Cook for 10 minutes (15 or more at high altitudes). Allow pressure to drop normally. Serve as above, and think of the energy you've saved.

FRIJOLES REFRITOS

Many people think that beans are at their best on the second day, when they are served as refried beans. **Philomena,** who has a well-known restaurant of the same name in Los Alamos, recommends this classic method. To 2 tablespoons bacon drippings add 2 cups day-old cooked pinto beans. Use a potato masher for mashing and stir-ring beans as they fry. When beans are thoroughly hot, add ¾ cup grated cheddar or jack cheese. Continue stirring until cheese has melted. Serve hot. Some New Mexicans also like to fry a small minced onion in the fat before adding the beans. Whatever method you use the resulting dish is delicious.

PREPARING FRESH CHILE

Select plump fresh New Mexico-grown chile pods, either green or red. The variety of the chile will determine how hot it is. (See "Chile— New Mexico's Fiery Soul" and the Nakayama Scale in *The Best from New Mexico Kitchens*.) New Mexico #6 and Anaheim are two of the mildest varieties, and Numex Big Jim rates #3 on a scale of 10. (The sizzling jalapeño is only #7!)

Slit pods lengthwise and remove seeds and veins, which make chiles far too hot for most palates. Place pods on a foil-lined cookie sheet under broiler. Or place pods on outdoor grill. Roast pods, turning frequently so they don't burn. When chile skins are blistered and loose, remove from fire (tongs would be handy for this) and cover with damp towels until cool. Peel skins from stem downward. Chiles are then ready to use or to freeze for the future. If you want to save your own skin from being blistered by the chiles, you had better wear thin rubber gloves while you work.

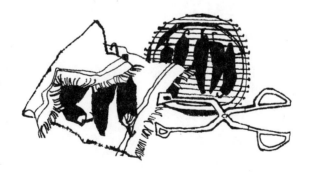

RED CHILE SAUCE I

This is Mark Nohl's traditional recipe made from whole dry red chile pods, the kind that hang on every door-side ristra in New Mexico or are bought in big plastic bags at supermarkets and roadside stands.

Wash and remove seeds, stems, and white veins (the more seeds and veins you leave in, the hotter the sauce will be). Place pods in a large kettle and cover with boiling water. Cook the pods until they become plump and tender. Remove pods and run them through your blender or processor (in the old days they used a food mill or fruit press). Strain the mixture to remove pieces of skin and stray seeds. Add some of the water you used to cook the pods in order to get the consistency of tomato paste. To this add 3 tablespoons fat, several cloves of minced garlic, 1 teaspoon dried oregano, and 1 teaspoon salt. Bring sauce to a boil, reduce heat, and simmer for about 45 minutes. This is your basic red chile sauce and is the smoothest you can make. To this you can add pinto beans, meat, onions, or tomatoes to construct your favorite New Mexico recipes, or use as is to go over burritos or enchilada plates.

RED CHILE SAUCE II

3 tablespoons olive oil or lard
1 clove garlic, minced
½ cup New Mexico chile powder
2 tablespoons flour
2 cups water
salt to taste

Saute the garlic in oil. Blend in flour and chile powder quickly with a wooden spoon. (Be careful not to burn the chile.) Blend in water and cook to desired consistency, adding more water as desired. If you have stock instead of water, so much the better. Add salt to taste.

GREEN CHILE SAUCE

¼ cup salad or olive oil
1 clove garlic, minced
½ cup minced onion (optional)
1 tablespoon flour
1 cup water
1 cup chopped green chile
salt to taste

Saute garlic and onion in oil in heavy saucepan. Blend in flour with wooden spoon. Add water and green chile and mix well. Add salt. Bring to a boil and simmer, stirring frequently, for 5 minutes.

THE OWL BAR'S GREEN CHILE

The Owl Bar & Cafe in San Antonio, south of Socorro, has become world-renowned—literally!—for its huge, juicy hamburgers. (It's been featured in *New Mexico Magazine*, TWA's *Ambassador Magazine* and the *Washington Post*.) But the cafe is also known for its atmosphere and its green chile. The secret, says Rowena Baca, the owner, is in the simmering.

3½ pounds hot green chile
1½ pounds hamburger meat
3 cloves garlic, minced
2 quarts water
salt to taste

Roast, peel, and dice green chile. In a heavy skillet, brown the meat and drain excess fat. In large heavy saucepan, cover chile and garlic with water and bring to boiling point. Mix in the meat and simmer, tightly covered, for at least 3 hours. Add salt to taste.

SALSA PHILOMENA

Here is the recipe from the famous **Philomena's** in Los Alamos. Instead of the crushed chile pequins (seeds), some cooks might use jalapeños.

1 can tomatoes (#303)
1 clove garlic, minced
½ teaspoon crushed chile pequins
½-1 teaspoon salt
¼ cup finely chopped onions
½ teaspoon oregano

Mash the canned tomatoes, add other ingredients, mix, and serve. Use on tacos, eggs, and hamburgers or as a dip for tostadas.

FLOUR TORTILLAS

2 cups flour
1 teaspoon salt
½ teaspoon baking powder (optional)
4 tablespoons lard
½-¾ cup lukewarm water

Mix dry ingredients, then work in lard until mixture is crumbly. Stir in the half cup of water, adding more if needed. Knead dough on a lightly floured board, then make into small balls, about the size of an egg. Let these stand covered by a tea towel for about 15 minutes. Then roll out to the size of a salad or luncheon plate. Bake on a hot, ungreased griddle for 2 minutes. Turn and bake for 1 minute on the other side. They should have a brown-freckled surface. Use immediately, or keep warm until serving by placing between the folds of a clean tea towel. If necessary, they may be refrigerated in plastic bags and reheated—but they're better when they're fresh.

DO-IT-YOURSELF TOSTADAS

Cut corn tortillas in quarters or eighths, depending on their size. Fry in at least ½ inch of corn oil until they are crisp. Drain on paper towels. Sprinkle with salt, garlic salt, and perhaps chile powder.

NACHOS

Nachos are educated tostadas. Prepare tostadas as above. Spread with frijoles refritos, a bit of minced onion, and a dash of chile powder or a piece of green chile. Sprinkle with grated cheddar cheese and maybe garlic salt. Heat in oven or broiler and serve.

JICAMA DIPPERS

The jicama is a potato-like vegetable with a crisp texture. Peel and cut a large jicama into ⅛-inch slices. Arrange on plate and sprinkle with lemon juice and salt. Use as dippers for bean dip, guacamole, or whatever you have.

GUACAMOLE LA TERTULIA

In *The Best from New Mexico Kitchens*, we gave you the recipe for this elegantly simple guacamole as made by the Santa Fe restaurant **La Tertulia**. We think it bears repeating.

1 ripe avocado
¼ teaspoon garlic salt
lettuce
corn chips or tostadas

Mash the avocado and mix in garlic salt. That's all there is to it. Serve on lettuce as a salad or in a bowl as a dip.

GUACAMOLE ESPAÑOLA

There's more bite per bite in this version.

2 ripe avocados
¼ teaspoon garlic salt
1 small tomato
1 tablespoon minced onion
2 tablespoons chopped green chile

Mash the avocados and mix in garlic salt. Finely chop the tomato and mix in along with onion and green chile. Add salt and pepper to taste—and more green chile and garlic if you like! Serve with corn chips or tostadas.

HOUMMUS B'TAHINI
(Chick Pea Dip)

Many newcomers are surprised to discover that New Mexico has a long-established Lebanese community. Second- and third-generation Lebanese cooks still prepare specialities from the ancestral homeland—right alongside chiles rellenos and carne adovada.

From Sam Adelo come these two Lebanese dips that could be served with Lebanese bread, pita bread, or even tostadas. Tahini is a sharp-tasting white sesame paste, not to be confused with the nutty brown Chinese variety. Tahini is usually available at good delicatessens or health food stores.

1 cup cooked or canned chick peas (garbanzos), drained
2 cloves garlic
¼ cup lemon juice
¾ cup tahini
salt and pepper to taste

Drain chick peas and reserve liquid. Press garlic into peas. Run chick peas in blender until smooth. Blend in lemon juice and tahini. Season with salt and pepper to taste and add more lemon juice if desired. If mixture seems too thick, mix in some of the reserved chick pea liquid.

EGGPLANT AND TAHINI DIP

1 large eggplant
¼ cup lemon juice
¼ cup tahini
2 cloves garlic
salt and pepper to taste

Bake eggplant in hot oven until it is soft—at least 20 minutes. Allow to cool. Peel carefully. Cut in chunks and put in blender or processor to puree. Add lemon juice and tahini and press in garlic. Blend well and season to taste. Serve with Lebanese bread or crackers.

POOR MAN'S CAVIAR

Here's a somewhat different version of eggplant dip, this one from Armenia.

1 large eggplant
2 small onions, minced
4 tablespoons olive oil
3 tablespoons tomato paste
3 tablespoons lemon juice
¼ teaspoon garlic salt
salt and pepper to taste

Bake the whole eggplant in a hot oven for 25 minutes or cook in a large pot of boiling water for 25 minutes. Cool, peel, cut in chunks and puree in blender or processor. In a large heavy frying pan, saute the onion in 1 tablespoon of the oil. When onion is transparent, add the eggplant and tomato paste. Mix well. Cook slowly, stirring frequently, and gradually add the rest of the oil. When mixture is quite thick and dry—it could take an hour—stir in lemon juice and seasonings. Chill well before serving. Serve with small crackers.

CURRIED LENTIL SPREAD

Legumes make popular dips and spreads because not only are they low in fat but they're high in protein and fiber. This one would be good with crackers or crisp raw vegetable sticks.

½ pound dried lentils
1 quart water
2 tablespoons butter
1 medium onion, finely chopped
4 teaspoons curry powder
3 tablespoons tomato paste
1 teaspoon lemon juice
salt and pepper to taste

Rinse, drain, and pick over lentils. Cover with water and simmer for 30 minutes or until lentils are tender. Puree in blender or processor. Saute the onion in the butter until translucent. Mix in curry powder. Add pureed lentils, tomato paste, powder, and lemon juice and mix smooth. Add salt and pepper to taste. Cool before serving.

ROSWELL BEAN DIP

This old favorite has a number of variations. We like this one.

2 cups refried beans
1 cup sour cream
¼ cup taco sauce

Mash beans well or run through blender. Mix in sour cream and taco sauce. Serve with corn chips or vegetable sticks. No taco sauce? Try chopped green chile. Or enchilada sauce. Or chile powder to taste. Or a minced jalapeño.

SOPA DE FRIJOLES NEGROS

Black bean soup is usually thought of as a Mexican or Caribbean dish, but New Mexicans, well aware of the value of beans in the diet, have added this to their multicultural cuisine.

1 cup dry black beans
8 cups cold water
2 tablespoons oil
1 onion, minced
2 cloves garlic, minced
dash of Tabasco sauce
2 tablespoons sherry
salt to taste

3 cups steamed white rice
⅔ cup minced sweet onion

Wash and pick over beans. Put in a large heavy saucepan, add water, and bring to a boil. Simmer, covered, for about 1½ hours. Saute onions and garlic in oil and add to beans. Simmer for 1 hour or until beans are tender. Puree beans in blender or processor. Season to taste with Tabasco, sherry, and salt. Return to pan and simmer for a few minutes until flavors blend. Correct seasoning and serve in bowls with steamed rice. Top with minced onion. Instead of using the rice, some New Mexicans prefer to cut 6 corn tortillas into thin strips, fry until crisp, drain, and serve on soup. Either way, it's delicious. Serves 6.

GREEN CHILE SOUP

If you plan ahead during the summer months, you can have bell peppers as well as green chiles in your freezer to use all winter long. Wash the bell peppers and cut off the stems. Simmer in boiling water in a covered pan for about 5 minutes. Drain, peel, cut in quarters, remove veins and seeds, and pop pieces into plastic bags to freeze. And here's a lovely green soup you can make summer or winter.

3 bell peppers
3 green chiles
1 small onion
4 cups chicken stock
2 tablespoons butter
2 tablespoons flour
1 cup cream or evaporated milk
salt and pepper to taste
sour cream

Prepare bell peppers (see above). Roast, peel, and clean the chiles. Cut up onion. Puree peppers, chiles, and onions in food processor or blender with 1 cup of the stock. Melt butter, blend in flour, gradually stir in chile mixture and chicken stock. Bring to a boil and simmer gently, stirring constantly, until soup is smooth. Blend in cream or undiluted evaporated milk. Heat through but do not boil. Add salt and pepper to taste. Serve topped with sour cream. Serves 6.

ROMAN WONTON SOUP

The speciality of a skier who lives near Eagle Nest, this hearty soup goes together in minutes.

1 15-ounce can ravioli
1 can beef bouillon
1½ cups water
1 cup tomato juice
¼ cup dry sherry
¼ teaspoon basil

Combine ingredients in a saucepan, being careful not to mash ravioli. Heat to boiling and simmer gently for about 5 minutes.

TOMATO EGG-DROP SOUP

We don't know the origin of this soup, but you might call it Southwestern Chinese. At any rate, it's as good as it is unusual.

2 tomatos
2 ounces cooked ham
3 cups chicken stock
2 teaspoons soy sauce
2 shallots, chopped
salt and pepper to taste
1 egg

Peel tomatoes and chop. Chop ham. Bring stock to a boil, add tomatoes and ham, then stir in soy sauce and chopped shallots. Add salt and pepper to taste. Bring to boil again. Stir in lightly beaten egg, and remove from heat immediately. Serves 3-4.

MOM'S MAGIC DOUGH

Fern Lyon, known for her witty book reviews, submits this recipe with her own inimitable directions.

2 packages dry yeast
2 cups warm water
½ cup sugar
¼ cup vegetable oil
½ teaspoon salt
1 beaten egg (optional)
6 cups flour (more or less)

Sprinkle yeast over warm water in large bowl. Stir until yeast is dissolved. Blend in sugar, oil, salt, and egg (if desired). Add 3 cups of flour and stir thoroughly with a wooden spoon. Add about 3 more cups of flour and turn out onto a smooth surface to knead. (Flour varies with weather conditions, type of flour, and signs of the zodiac. Experiment.) Knead mixture until you have worked off all your aggressions and the dough is smooth. Shape the dough into a ball and put it into a buttered bowl in a warm place (top of refrigerator, maybe, or the oven that has been barely warmed) and cover with a towel or loose lid. Let it rise to about double its original size, which should take about 2 hours. It varies.

Punch risen dough down and (1) put into refrigerator for about 24 hours, (2) let it rise another ½ hour. Then make into rolls, sweet rolls, cinnamon rolls, bread, or pizza bottoms. This also makes good fry bread, doughnuts, or sopaipillas, if you don't mind fooling around with deep fat.

If you've made your dough into rolls or loaves, put them in well-greased pans and let rise one more hour or until they are almost the size you want. Bake at about 375 degrees F for 25-30 minutes for rolls, about 50 minutes for bread. (The time will depend on your stove, the weather, and again, the zodiac, or something.) This recipe will make 2 loaves of bread.

SAN JUAN COUNTY SPOON BREAD

1 quart milk
1 cup yellow cornmeal
1 cup butter or margarine, melted
1 teaspoon salt
1 teaspoon sugar
4 eggs, separated
¼ cup minced onion
1 4-ounce can chopped green chile, drained

Heat milk over hot water. Gradually add cornmeal, stirring constantly. Cook until thick and mushy. Remove from heat and stir in butter, salt, and sugar. Beat egg whites stiff and set aside. Beat egg yolks thick in a large bowl. Slowly mix in cornmeal mixture, then onion and chile. Fold in egg whites. Turn into a greased 2-quart baking dish, set dish in a pan of hot water, and bake at 325 degrees F for one hour or until firm.

BLUE CORNBREAD

Lani Gaskill has adapted blue cornmeal to the traditional cornbread recipe and come up with a winner.

1½ cups blue cornmeal
3 tablespoons sugar
2 teaspoons baking powder
¾ cup milk
1 beaten egg
3 tablespoons bacon fat, melted
¼ cup crumbled bacon
1 4-ounce can chopped green chile

Combine first 3 ingredients. Mix the balance of the ingredients in another bowl. Combine and mix until just moist. Pour into greased 8-inch square pan and bake at 350 degrees F for 30 minutes or until done.

CHILE BREAD

Here's a surprising raised dough ring that will make chile lovers wake up and sing. Glenna Rose Autrey of Santa Fe dreamed it up.

1 package dry yeast
¼ cup warm water
4½ cups flour
½ cup melted butter
1 cup warm milk
¼ cup sugar
1 teaspoon salt
1 egg

1½ cups finely chopped onion
½ cup melted butter
3 tablespoons red chile powder
   or ½ cup chopped green chile

Dissolve yeast in water. Mix in 2 cups of the flour, butter, milk, sugar, salt, and egg. Beat for 2 minutes. Add enough flour to make a stiff dough. Turn onto a floured board and knead until smooth. Put in a greased bowl, turn over, and cover with a clean cloth. Put bowl in a warm place with no drafts and let dough rise until doubled—about 1 hour.

Combine remaining ingredients for filling. Punch dough down and roll into a 20 x 8 inch rectangle. Cut into four 20 x 2 inch strips. Spread filling on each strip and fold over lengthwise. Twist 2 strips together, then twist double strips together and form in a circle on greased cookie sheet. Cover with clean cloth and let rise until doubled. Brush with beaten egg and sprinkle with chile powder. Bake at 350 degrees F for 40 minutes.

ZUCCHINI NUT BREAD

3 eggs
2 cups sugar
3 teaspoons vanilla
1 cup safflower or other vegetable oil
2 cups grated unpeeled zucchini
2 cups flour
1 cup whole wheat flour
¼ teaspoon baking powder
1 teaspoon bicarbonate of soda
2 teaspoons cinnamon
½ teaspoon nutmeg
1 cup chopped pecans

Grease and flour 2 loaf tins. Set oven at 350 degrees F. Beat eggs light
and foamy, then gradually beat in sugar. Continue beating and add
vanilla and oil. Stir in grated zucchini. Sift in dry ingredients and
fold in gently. Fold in pecans. Bake for 1-1¼ hours. Cool on wire racks.

SWEDISH PANCAKES

Lucy Jelinek-Thompson, a freelance graphic artist, brought this recipe
from her home state of Wisconsin. Lucy and her husband, who live
in an earth-sheltered passive solar house near Santa Fe, make these
pancakes almost every Sunday morning.

4 eggs
3 cups milk
3 teaspoons sugar
1½ cups flour
1 teaspoon salt
2 tablespoons butter, melted

Beat eggs. Add milk and dry ingredients alternately, mixing well. Slowly
stir in melted butter. Bake on medium-hot griddle, flipping when
golden. Serve with lingonberries, syrup, or honey. Serves 6.

AVOCADOS

Select ripe avocados. Allow ½ avocado per person and serve on the half shell with only a drizzle of oil-and-vinegar dressing. And a spoon, of course.

Guacamole (see page 12) may be served as a salad. Spoon it over shredded lettuce.

SUNLAND SALAD

2 navel oranges
2 ripe avocados
1 large sweet onion (Spanish or Bermuda)
oil-and-vinegar dressing
1 tablespoon minced green onions

Peel oranges, removing all white pith, and slice in thin circles. Peel and slice avocados. Peel and slice onion in thin slices. On a glass plate, arrange rings of alternating overlapping slices of orange, avocado, and onion. Drizzle with dressing, sprinkle with green onions, and chill before serving. A beautiful sight on a warm summer day. Serves 4.

MANUELITA'S BEAN POT

Manuelita Romero of Nambé has a highly individual way with baked beans.

2 16-ounce cans kidney beans
2 tablespoons bacon fat
2 teaspoons dry mustard
1 bay leaf
2 crushed cloves
2 cloves garlic, crushed
¼ teaspoon thyme
¼ teaspoon rosemary
¼ cup pickle syrup (from watermelon or peach pickles)
salt and pepper to taste
2 onion slices
6 bacon slices
¼ cup black coffee
4 jiggers blended whiskey

Mix beans, bacon fat, mustard, bay leaf, cloves, garlic, thyme, rosemary, pickle syrup, and salt and pepper to taste. Bake in a bean pot at 350 degrees F for 1 hour. Separate onion slices into rings and arrange on beans. Put bacon slices on top. Bake 30 minutes longer. Pour coffee and whiskey over beans. Serves 6-8.

FLYING X CHUCKWAGON BARBECUE BEANS

The Flying X Chuckwagon near Carlsbad is known far and wide for its big family-style dinners and entertainment. They admit that they don't know how to cook in small batches—this recipe will serve 175 people, so save it for the family reunion or the church supper.

8 cans pinto beans (industrial size, drained)
2 cups Grandma's molasses
2 cups brown sugar
2 handfuls dried onion flakes
2 tablespoons salt
2 tablespoons black pepper
½ gallon tomato sauce
1 quart commercial chile sauce

Put this in a 350-degree F oven—if you have a pot and an oven big enough!—and bake for about 4 hours or so, stirring every half hour or so. You'll probably have to add a little water as you go along, so the mixture doesn't dry out.

CHAYOTES

The chayote, a pale green squash-like vegetable, a member of the cucumber family, has left its native Mexico and is now grown and eaten all over the world. In the South Pacific and Australasia, where it is known as the choko, it has become almost as popular as zucchini. The chayote has a bland flavor and takes happily to savory seasonings (bacon, garlic, chile, whatever). It also holds its shape well when cooked.

You can boil or steam the whole chayote, then peel and cube to use in other dishes. (Actually, you don't HAVE to peel it.) Serve it mashed with butter, salt, and pepper. Chill the cubes and toss in a salad—or toss them in raw for a delicate crunchy treat. Saute cubes or slices in butter and mix with scrambled eggs. Hollow out a steamed chayote, mash the flesh and mix with creamed curried crab, then serve in chayote halves. Well, you'll think of other ideas.

JICAMA

The jicama is a large brown root vegetable with a crisp apple-like white flesh. It is frequently used instead of water chestnuts. Peel it and eat it raw or cooked. It's an excellent addition to salads. Try it cut up with cucumbers, onions, and oranges and tossed with oil-and-vinegar dressing.

FRIJOLES
(See pages 5, 6)

CRUCES CHRISTMAS SALAD

4 beets, cooked or canned, diced
2 peeled navel oranges, sliced and quartered
2 cups raw jicama cubes
1 cup pineapple chunks, fresh or canned (drained)
2 peeled bananas, sliced
½ head lettuce, shredded
½ cup oil-and-vinegar dressing
seeds of 1 pomegranate
½ cup chopped Portales peanuts

Put beets, oranges, jicama cubes,pineapple chunks, and bananas in a glass bowl on a bed of shredded lettuce. Pour dressing over all. Sprinkle with pomegranate seeds and peanuts. Serve.

CHINESE COLESLAW

2 cups finely shredded Chinese cabbage
½ cup chopped parsley
½ cup well-drained canned crushed pineapple
½ cup sliced drained canned water chestnuts (or jicama)
2 green onions, chopped
¼ cup coleslaw dressing
¼ teaspoon fresh grated ginger

Combine in a salad bowl cabbage, parsley, pineapple, water chestnuts (or fresh peeled and sliced jicama),and onions. Cover and chill well. Combine dressing and ginger, pour over salad, toss well, and serve. Serves 4-6.

ELOTES ASADOS
(Broiled Corn on the Cob)

Carlos Martínez says this is the ONLY way to cook corn on the cob: Soak desired quantities of *elotes* overnight in water, husk and all. [I think you could pull down the husks, remove the silk, and then replace husks.—SMC] Place *elotes* on grid over coals. Turn when husk chars a little. The water that has been absorbed by the husk steams, making your *elote* tender and juicy. Dip in garlic butter and ¡wow! A great complement to your meat and good for any outing.

CORNFETTI SALAD

Here's one to take to the next potluck supper or barbecue.

3 cups cooked or canned corn niblets
½ cup chopped bell pepper
2 tablespoons minced onion
1 tablespoon chopped parsley
¼ cup chopped pimiento
¼ cup chopped green chile
1 beef stock cube, crushed
1 tablespoon red wine vinegar
⅓ cup mayonnaise
2 tablespoons sour cream
salt and pepper to taste
6 slices bacon, fried and crumbled

Combine corn, pepper, onion, parsley, pimiento, and chile in serving bowl and chill. Dissolve stock cube in vinegar. Mix into mayonnaise along with sour cream. Toss gently with corn mixture and add salt and pepper as needed. Just before serving, sprinkle with bacon crumbles and toss again. Serves 6.

EGGPLANT WITH MOZZARELLA

This is one of the nicest things that's ever happened to an eggplant. Try it and see if you don't agree. The recipe comes from Las Vegas, from a representative of New Mexico's large Italian-American population.

1 small eggplant
4 ounces mozzarella cheese
1 tablespoon chopped chives
1 large tomato
salt and pepper to taste
oil for deep frying

½ cup flour
½ cup cornstarch
½ teaspoon salt
1 teaspoon baking powder
¾ cup water
1 egg white

Cut unpeeled eggplant into ½-inch slices, then cut again into ¼-inch slices, but not all the way. You should have 2 flaps of eggplant with a "hinge" on the side. Cut mozzarella into thin slices and insert one in each eggplant envelope. Cut tomato into thin slices, sprinkle each with chives and salt and pepper, and insert into eggplant envelope. Holding eggplant cases together with tongs, dip into prepared batter, then into hot oil. Fry until golden brown and drain on paper towels. *Batter*: Sift flour, cornstarch, salt, and baking powder into a bowl. Gradually stir in water until smooth. Beat egg white stiff and fold in.

GREEK SALAD

½ head lettuce
18 radishes
¼ pound feta cheese, crumbled
1 small can drained anchovy filets, minced
2 tomatoes, cut in small pieces
¼ cup fresh parsley, minced
½ cup sliced pitted ripe olives
¼ teaspoon dried oregano
pepper
1 bunch green onions, sliced
½ cup herbed oil-and-vinegar dressing

Tear lettuce into small pieces. Add remaining ingredients except dressing, toss lightly, and cover with a damp cloth. Chill for 1-2 hours. To serve, toss with dressing.

NOPALITOS
(See page 121)

SPAGHETTI SQUASH

The spaghetti squash, a seeming oddity, was taken to heart—or stomach—by New Mexicans almost as soon as it was introduced. And why not? The Southwest is a natural homeland of pumpkins, gourds, and squashes, and this one is unique in appearance, crunchy in texture, and delicious to the taste. Serve it plain, with butter, salt, and pepper, or with any number of sauces, including, naturally, green chile sauce. Or, how about the version below?

WEIGHT-WATCHING "SPAGHETTI"

1 3-pound spaghetti squash
2 tablespoons olive oil
2 cloves garlic, minced
1 pound mushrooms, sliced
1 cup red wine
2 cups tomato sauce
¼ teaspoon oregano
salt and pepper to taste
tomato juice, V-8 or water
grated parmesan cheese

To cook the squash, cover with water, bring to a boil, and simmer 5 minutes. Turn over and continue simmering another 5 minutes. Remove from water, cut in half lengthwise and discard seeds and tough strings in center. Place halves cut side down in about 2 inches of water. Cover and simmer for about 15 minutes, or until tender. Don't overcook—you want it crisp, not mushy. With 2 forks, loosen up the "spaghetti" strands. *Sauce:* Saute garlic in olive oil. Add mushrooms and saute 5 minutes. Add wine, tomato sauce, oregano, salt, and pepper, and mix well. Bring to a boil, cover, and simmer for about 30 minutes. If sauce is too thick stir in additional water, tomato juice, or V-8 as it cooks. Serve over spaghetti squash and sprinkle with grated parmesan cheese.

RÍO GRANDE SPINACH SALAD

½ pound young spinach
1 small tomato
4 hard-boiled eggs
½ onion
⅓ cup crumbled feta cheese
2 tablespoons olive oil
1 tablespoon wine vinegar
¼ teaspoon dried oregano
¼ teaspoon freshly ground pepper
¼ cup ripe olives, pitted and sliced

Clean spinach well and tear into small pieces. Cut tomato in wedges
and arrange over spinach. Cut eggs in quarters and arrange on top.
Cut onion into slices and separate into rings over spinach. Crumble
feta cheese over all. Shake olive oil, vinegar, oregano, and pepper in
a small jar and drizzle over salad. Sprinkle with olive slices. Toss and
serve.

CALABACITAS

This is probably the best-known vegetable dish in New Mexico, and every cook has a version of it. Some don't use corn, others use bell peppers, and a few (horrors!) don't use green chile.

2 tablespoons oil
1 clove garlic, minced
1 medium onion, chopped
1 pound zucchini, cut up
1 12-ounce can niblet corn, drained
2 medium tomatoes, peeled and chopped
½ cup chopped green chile
salt to taste
½ cup grated cheddar, jack, or longhorn cheese

Saute the garlic, onion, and zucchini in oil until onion becomes translucent. Mix in well-drained corn, tomatoes, and chile. Cover tightly and heat through. Add salt to taste and, just before serving, mix cheese in lightly. Serves 4.

ITALIAN ZUCCHINI

2 medium-large zucchini
2 eggs
1 tablespoon water
salt and pepper
2 tablespoons grated parmesan cheese
½ cup flour
½ cup olive oil

Clean zucchini and cut in ¼-inch slices. Beat eggs and water together well. Add salt and pepper and parmesan cheese. Dip zucchini slices in flour, then into egg mixture. Fry in oil until they are golden brown on each side. Drain on paper towels. Serve.

QUICHE D'HIER

Yesterday's vegetables, the lonely tomato, the solitary zucchini, become gourmet fare in this dish.

⅔ cup flour
⅔ cup whole wheat flour
½ teaspoon baking powder
1 teaspoon chile powder
½ cup butter
⅔ cup grated cheddar cheese

⅔ cup cream
2 eggs
1-1½ cups lightly cooked vegetables
1 tablespoon minced onion
salt and pepper to taste
extra grated cheese (optional)

Combine flour, whole wheat flour, baking powder, and chile powder and cut in butter until mixture is crumbly. Mix in cheese. Add about 2 tablespoons cold water to make a pastry dough. Lightly roll out pastry and fit into a 9-inch deep pie or flan pan. Bake at 350 degrees F for about 15 minutes. Beat cream and eggs together. Add well-drained vegetables: chopped zucchini, corn niblets, chopped tomato, small broccoli spears, cauliflower flowerets, chopped spinach, chopped green chile, or whatever else you have on hand, along with the minced onion. Add salt and pepper to taste and turn mixture into pie shell. Sprinkle with more grated cheese, if you like. Bake for 35 minutes at 350 degrees F, or until filling has set. Serves 4.

FETTUCCINE ALFREDO

In **Trudy's Restaurant,** formerly in Las Vegas and now in Raton, this noodle dish is a speciality.

1 pound spinach noodles
1 pint (2 cups) whipping cream
8 ounces real Swiss cheese, grated
½ cup grated parmesan cheese (a "generous handful")
freshly ground black pepper

Trudy insists on the spinach noodles for their color and body. If your supermarket doesn't carry them, try a health food store or gourmet delicatessen. Drop noodles in rapidly boiling salted water. While they are cooking, combine the cream and cheeses and heat over very low burner. When the cheese has melted and the sauce is hot—but not boiling—pour over noodles, which have been cooked tender, rinsed in cold water and then rinsed in hot water. Sprinkle with freshly ground pepper and serve.

MEXICAN RICE

¼ cup vegetable oil
1 clove garlic, minced
¼ cup minced onion
1 cup uncooked long-grain rice
1 tomato, peeled and chopped
1 cup tomato juice
1½ cups chicken stock or water
½ cup chopped bell pepper
¼ cup chopped green chile
salt to taste

Saute garlic and onion in vegetable oil until translucent. Stir in rice and allow to turn golden. Add remaining ingredients and mix well. Cover tightly and cook until rice is tender and liquid has been absorbed. Stir occasionally during the cooking.

MESILLA VERMICELLI

8 ounces vermicelli
½ cup vegetable oil
1 tablespoon minced onion
1 cup chopped peeled fresh tomatoes
1 cup sliced mushrooms
1½ cups chicken stock
salt and pepper to taste
½ cup grated cheddar cheese

Break up the vermicelli while it's still in the bag. In a large heavy saucepan, saute the vermicelli in oil, turning frequently, until golden brown. Add onion, tomatoes, mushrooms,and chicken stock. Mix well, bring to a boil, season to taste. Cover tightly and simmer until vermicelli is tender and liquid has all been absorbed—20-25 minutes. If necessary, add more stock during the cooking. Sprinkle with grated cheese before serving.

TACOS

Heat or quickly fry corn tortillas until soft. Fold over. Have your fillings ready. Try hot refried beans seasoned with a bit of garlic, minced raw onion, and thin strips of jack or cheddar cheese. Or use chopped chicken, pork, or beef mixed with some homemade chile sauce or commercial taco sauce and heated. Or use strips of fresh or canned green chile and fingers of jack or cheddar cheese. Place tacos on a tray or ovenproof plates and pop into the oven to keep warm and to melt the cheese. When serving, add shredded lettuce, chopped tomatoes, chopped onion, and/or sliced avocado. And pass the hot sauce.

FLAUTAS

Anything that works for a taco can work for a flauta (flute), which is an upmarket taco. Heat your corn tortillas on an ungreased griddle, fill with a tablespoon or so of any of the above mixtures or whatever else appeals to you, roll up and pin securely with a wooden toothpick. Fry in oil until lightly browned. Drain on paper towels. Allow 3 per serving and top with guacamole.

BURRITOS

The "little donkey" is a New Mexico sandwich—a flour tortilla filled with refried beans and whatever else you like. Heat the tortilla on an ungreased griddle, spread with hot refried beans, sprinkle with hot sauce, add onions and/or chile and/or cheese as desired. Fold up ends and roll so you have a closed envelope (to help keep the goodness from dripping out on your arms or lap). Use a toothpick if necessary to hold it closed. Pick up and eat.

GREEN CHILE STEW

1½ pounds lean stew beef or shank
1 large onion, chopped
2 cloves garlic, minced
2 tablespoons cooking oil
4 cups water (use ½ cup white wine if desired)
½-1 cup chopped green chile
4 potatoes, quartered
4 zucchini, cut in chunks
1 small potato, grated
salt and pepper to taste

Cut beef in small cubes. Brown with onion and garlic in oil. Add water and green chile. Cook in slow cooker for several hours or until beef is getting tender. Add potatoes, zucchini, and grated potato. Add salt and pepper to taste. Simmer or slow-cook until vegetables are soft and meat is tender. If you want the mixture to be thicker, stir in a flour-and-butter roux. Serve in soup bowls with warm tortillas. Serves 4.

POSOLE SANDOVAL

Posole is whole hominy, and in New Mexico it is cooked with pork into a thick stew. The first time you taste it, you may be unimpressed. The second time, well, you think that perhaps another helping would go down well. The third time—you're hooked. Like the rest of us, you won't think that Christmas Eve or a feast day of any kind is complete without a big bowl of steaming posole. Richard C. Sandoval, who grew up in Nambé, prepares his holiday posole this way. Richard uses frozen posole, but if you can't find that, perhaps you can find dried posole. Failing that, you might make do with canned hominy, which, of course, won't need to cook as long as the other varieties. But, as Richard points out, it won't taste as good, either!

2 pounds frozen posole
2 pounds pork roast, cut up
dash of oregano
3-4 dry red chile pods, broken up
salt to taste

Rinse posole well. Put posole, oregano, and chile pods in a large pot. Add cold water to about 2 inches above the corn. Heat to a boil and cook for 20 minutes. Add the meat, reduce heat, and simmer for about 3 hours, until meat is cooked and kernels are soft but not mushy. (You might need less time at lower altitudes than Santa Fe's.) Stir frequently and add water as needed. Salt to taste at end. Serve in bowls and pass the chile sauce. Or use as an accompaniment to a dinner of enchiladas, tamales, frijoles, and chiles rellenos.

TORTILLA HASH

If you can't find chorizos in your market, don't despair. Use the Silver City Sausage recipe on page 62. Take a pound of it, crumble in a heavy skillet, and fry until it is well done, about 30 minutes. Drain and use as below.

12 corn tortillas
vegetable oil
1 pound chorizos
1 cup minced onion
2 tablespoons chile powder
2 cups tomato sauce
½ pound jack cheese, grated
1 cup sliced ripe olives
½ cup grated parmesan cheese

Cut tortillas in eighths and fry in vegetable oil. Don't allow to brown. Drain on paper towels. Remove chorizo casings and slice the sausage thinly. Fry in same oil and set aside on paper towels to drain. Pour away remaining fat. Fry onions in a teaspoonful of fresh oil until they are translucent. Mix in tomato sauce and chile powder and heat thoroughly. In a casserole, put alternate layers of tortillas, jack cheese, olives, and chorizo. Pour the sauce over all. Sprinkle with parmesan cheese. Bake for about 30 minutes at 350 degrees F. Serves 8-10.

NEW MEXICO ENCHILADAS

Heat blue corn tortillas in hot oil and drain. Layer tortillas on oven-proof plates, allowing at least 3 per person, with grated cheddar or longhorn cheese, minced raw onion, and red or green chile sauce. Top the stack with a fried egg and serve.

CHOPE'S CHILES RELLENOS

One of the most popular spots in southern New Mexico is **Chope's Cafe & Bar** in La Mesa. José Benavides, whose family has lived in the Mesilla Valley for six generations, is owner of the restaurant. The 100-year-old adobe building has been a restaurant for more than 50 years. You'll see why when you taste these chiles rellenos.

12 firm, long green chiles
1 pound yellow longhorn cheese
2 cups pure lard
¾ cup flour
4 eggs, separated

Roast and peel the chiles. Cut the cheese into 12 strips about 3 or 4 inches long and ½ inch thick. Make a slit about an inch long near the top of each chile and insert a cheese strip. Roll the chile in the flour and set aside. Melt the lard in a large skillet to medium hot. (If your skillet has a thermostat, try no hotter than 350 degrees F.) Beat the egg whites until they form peaks. Beat the egg yolks and then mix into whites. Dip the floured chiles into egg until well coated, then fry in lard until golden brown. (If lard is too hot, the egg will burn, so be careful.) Drain well and serve warm.

CARNE ADOVADA

Marinate lean pork chops, pork steaks, or loin of pork in red chile sauce overnight. Bake pork, basting occasionally with more sauce, at 350 degrees F for 1-2 hours, or until done. Time will depend on the thickness of the cut you are using.

HUEVOS RANCHEROS

When you're perishing for a taste of New Mexico and there's "not a decent restaurant" for 100 miles, it's time for a do-it-yourself cure. Canned or frozen green chile and tortillas are available in most parts of the United States and in many surprising places abroad. Huevos rancheros are good at breakfast, brunch, lunch, supper—well, almost any time you're hungry for them.

1 clove garlic, minced
1 large onion, chopped
1 bell pepper, chopped
2 medium tomatoes, chopped
2-6 tablespoons chopped green chile
2 tablespoons bacon fat
1 teaspoon chicken stock base
salt and pepper to taste
6 corn tortillas
3 tablespoons corn oil
6 eggs
1 cup grated cheese, jack or cheddar

Saute the garlic, onion, pepper, tomatoes, and chile in bacon fat. Season with stock base and salt and pepper to taste. Simmer until slightly thickened. Fry tortillas quickly in hot corn oil—don't allow them to get hard. Drain on paper towels. Fry eggs carefully in same oil. Gently slip an egg onto each tortilla. Top with sauce. Allow at least 2 eggs per person. Sprinkle with grated cheese and serve immediately. Serves 3.

CHIMICHANGA

Anyone who's familiar with Los Alamos knows **Philomena's Restaurant.** Housed in the old gatehouse (now expanded with a spacious glassed-in *sala* with views of the spectacular mountain ranges of northern New Mexico), the restaurant has served local residents, tourists, nuclear physicists, and international movers and shakers. One of Philomena Romero's most often requested dishes is the delightful chimichanga—slang for "monkeying around."

For each serving:
1 warm flour tortilla
2 tablespoons hot refried beans
1 tablespoon chopped green chile
2 tablespoons grated longhorn cheese
3 tablespoons commercial sour cream
2 tablespoons guacamole
salsa
shredded lettuce
chopped tomatoes

On center of warm tortilla, spread refried beans and chile and sprinkle with cheese. Fold edges of tortilla to the center, overlapping. Place finished side down on serving plate. Spread sour cream across the top and guacamole on top of that. Spoon salsa on the ends. Garnish with lettuce and tomatoes. Eat. Philomena cautions that the filling must be stove-hot so that the cheese will melt. The plate should be hot, too. And, as Philomena says, you can monkey around with the filling to suit yourself.

MEXICAN PIZZA

Well, maybe this isn't *authentic*—but that doesn't stop it from tasting good!

1½ cups flour
½ cup yellow cornmeal
3 teaspoons baking powder
½ teaspoon salt
⅓ cup shortening
¾ cup milk

1 pound ground beef
1 clove garlic, minced
¼ teaspoon salt
1 15-ounce can refried beans
1 4-ounce can chopped green chile
1 9-ounce jar or can taco sauce
3 green onions, sliced
2 cups shredded cheese, jack or cheddar

Mix flour, cornmeal, baking powder, and salt. Cut in shortening until mixture is crumbly. Mix in milk with fork until dough forms. Turn dough onto floured board and knead until smooth. Roll into 13-inch circle and place on ungreased cookie sheet or pizza tin. Pinch edge to form 1-inch rim. Heat oven to 400 degrees F. Meanwhile, cook beef and garlic in a skillet, breaking up meat into bits. When meat is lightly browned, drain off excess fat. Spread pizza dough with beans, then spread with meat mixture. Layer on green chile, then taco sauce. Sprinkle with onions. Pour over taco sauce. Top with cheese. Bake for about 20 minutes, or until crust is golden brown and cheese bubbling.

PERFECT FRIED FISH

This is an international recipe—the cooking method comes from the Department of Fisheries in Canada and the batter comes from a famous fish restaurant, Doyle's, in Sydney. If you follow the directions, your fish will be moist and succulent with a thin crispy coating. And everyone will want to know your secret. Just remember, the fish must be absolutely FRESH.

½ cup flour
1 cup water
any fish or filet as long as it is very, very fresh
vegetable oil

Mix the flour with half the water in a bowl and begin beating it with a hand-held rotary beater (or electric beater at slow to medium speed). Gradually add the remaining water, beating constantly. Keep the beater moving as you do this, until the mixture has become smooth and has sufficient body to lightly adhere to a wooden spoon. If it seems too thick, do not hesitate to add a bit more water. When the batter is ready, it will drop back to the bowl very slowly from a spoon. Heat oil in deep fryer to 375 degrees F. Now *measure* your fish at its thickest point. For every 1-inch thickness, you cook the fish exactly 10 minutes. If the fish is ½-inch thick, cook it 5 minutes; if it's 2½ inches thick, cook it 25 minutes. Dip the fish into the batter, lower gently into the oil, and fry. Don't cook too many at once, as you will lower the temperature of the oil. Allow the temperature to come back up to 375 for each batch. Drain on paper towels and serve to delighted eaters.

HERBED FISH FILETS

4 large fish filets (flounder, sole, etc.)
⅓ cup slivered almonds
1 cup cornflakes
¼ teaspoon garlic powder
¼ cup grated parmesan cheese
⅓ cup chopped parsley
1 tablespoon minced chives
½ teaspoon paprika
salt and pepper
flour
2 eggs
vegetable oil
1 lemon

Toast almonds in moderate oven for about 5 minutes. Cool and chop fine. In a bowl, combine almonds, crushed cornflakes, garlic, parmesan cheese, parsley, chives, paprika, salt, and pepper. Mix well. Lightly beat eggs. Dip fish in flour, shake off excess, then dip in eggs. Coat fish on both sides with cornflake mixture, pressing crumbs on lightly. Heat oil in a large skillet for shallow frying. Cook fish on both sides until golden brown and cooked through. Serve with lemon wedges. Serves 4.

PRAWNS IN PERNOD

20 large fresh prawns (shrimp)
¼ cup butter
1 tablespoon finely chopped shallots
2 teaspoons minced fresh dill
1 small bell pepper, seeded and cut in slivers
¼ cup Pernod

Remove shells and veins from prawns. Pat dry with paper towels. Melt butter in a large skillet and saute the shallots, dill, and bell pepper for a few minutes. Add the prawns and toss. They will cook very quickly. Mix in the Pernod and serve immediately with rice.

LORN'S CHILE PRAWNS

A New Mexico architect whose hobby is Oriental cooking has provided this spicy Chinese recipe.

1½ pounds fresh prawns (large shrimp)
2 tablespoons oil
2 teaspoons minced fresh root ginger
1 clove garlic, minced
4 green onions, sliced diagonally
2 small red chile pods, seeded and finely chopped
1 bell pepper, preferably red, seeded and cut in chunks
1 tablespoon soy sauce
⅓ cup chicken stock
1 teaspoon cornstarch

Remove shells and veins from prawns. Pat dry with paper towels. Heat oil in a wok and stir-fry the prawns until they begin to turn pink, about 2 minutes. Remove from pan and keep in a warm place. Add a little more oil to the wok if necessary and stir-fry ginger, garlic, onions, chile and bell pepper for a minute or so, until they heat through. Add soy sauce and chicken stock. Bring to a boil. Mix cornstarch with a little cold water until smooth and add to the wok. Cook only until sauce boils and thickens. Add the prawns and cook only long enough to heat through. Serve hot with rice. Serves 4.

CRÊPES

This basic crêpe recipe can be used for any meal. Serve with preserves or with confectioners' sugar and lemon juice at breakfast or for dessert. Fill with meat mixtures for lunch or dinner.

1 cup flour
1 cup milk
¼ teaspoon salt
2 large eggs
1 teaspoon vegetable oil or melted butter
1 tablespoon brandy (for sweet pancakes)

Blend all the ingredients together—the easiest way is with a blender or processor. Set aside in refrigerator for at least an hour. Drop by spoonful on hot greased crêpe pan or heavy frying pan. Tilt pan so mixture spreads thin. These will cook very quickly, so be careful. Flip over and cook on other side. Don't allow them to get stiff or dry. Wrap in foil and keep warm in a slow oven while you prepare filling.

ITALIAN CRÊPES

16-24 small crêpes
1 pound ricotta cheese
1½ cups grated parmesan cheese
¼ cup chopped parsley
2 eggs
1 clove garlic, minced
½ cup butter, melted

Blend together ricotta, 1 cup of the parmesan, parsley, eggs, and garlic. Put 1 or 2 spoonfuls in the center of each crêpe, fold up ends, and roll into small packages. Put into baking dish, pour melted butter over all and sprinkle with remaining parmesan cheese. Cover and bake for 30 minutes at 375 degrees F. Serves 4-6.

HAM AND MUSHROOM CRÊPES

Lunch, of course—but think what a marvelous brunch this also would make!

8 crêpes
1 pound mushrooms
1 tablespoon minced onion
1 tablespoon butter
1 teaspoon chicken stock powder
dash of pepper
½ cup sour cream
2 teaspoons cornstarch
8 thin slices ham

Prepare crêpes and keep warm wrapped in foil in slow oven. Clean and slice mushrooms. Saute onion in butter. Add mushrooms and sprinkle with stock powder and pepper. Saute mushrooms but don't overcook them. Mix cornstarch in a little cold water (or dry sherry) and stir in with sour cream. Stir well and heat through but do not allow to boil. If mixture is too thick, add more sour cream. To serve, lay a slice of ham on each crêpe, allowing 2 per person. Use warm plates. Spoon mushroom filling on top, fold crêpes over, and serve at once. Serves 4.

CANNELLONI CRÊPES

18-24 small crêpes
1 cup cooked spinach
2 eggs
1¼ cups parmesan cheese
1½ cups cubed cooked meat (chicken, pork, or veal)
2 cups prepared spaghetti sauce (meat or mushroom)
salt and pepper to taste

Cool spinach slightly and drain well. Put spinach, eggs, 1 cup of the cheese, and the meat in processor and blend smooth. Put spoonfuls of filling into the center of crêpes, fold up ends, and roll into little packages. Put into a baking dish. Heat spaghetti sauce and pour over all. Sprinkle with the remaining parmesan cheese. Bake at 375 degrees F for about 30 minutes, or until crêpes are heated through. Serves 6.

ROAST BEEF ROLLUPS

Crêpes again—this time with leftover roast beef in a supremely easy dish.

8 large crêpes
2 onions, minced
2 tablespoons butter or margarine
8 thin slices roast beef
salt and pepper to taste
1 cup sour cream
1 tablespoon horseradish

Prepare your crêpes and keep warm. Saute the onion in butter until lightly browned. On each crêpe place a slice of roast beef. Sprinkle with onion, season with salt and pepper, and roll up. Place in a large flat baking dish. Mix sour cream and horseradish and spread over crêpes. Cover dish with lid or foil and bake at 360 degrees F for 10 minutes or until hot. Serves 4.

CABRITO

Cabrito is goat—and in New Mexico, that usually means a fiesta. Although goat is popular all around the globe, from France to Greece, from Africa to the Philippines, most North Americans aren't familiar with it. You don't usually find it in your neighborhood supermarket in plastic packages! Goat tastes quite a lot like lamb—but better, say its aficionados. But let's have Richard C. Sandoval, editor of *New Mexico Magazine*, and John Crenshaw, editor of *New Mexico Wildlife*, tell how they went about their cabrito barbecue:

First you have to get your goat. Ask people who raise goats, a butcher, friends, or perhaps meat packing houses. A kid four to six months old is about the right size. With luck, the seller will slaughter it for you. Otherwise, you'll have to do it yourself or take it to a commercial slaughterhouse.

Then it's time for fiesta, friends, family, good food, and lots of fun. And the more help you have, the more fun you can have. Needed in preparation for the actual roasting of the cabrito are some willing pit diggers and plenty of beer. For the party described, we had two strong, willing diggers and two not-so-willing butchers—and lots of beer.

We slaughtered the two goats on the eve before the roast. It's good to let the meat hang overnight in a cool place. We dug a pit approximately 3 feet wide by 5 feet long and 3 feet deep, and we lined the bottom with rocks. Then we piled apple tree prunings and large applewood logs inside the pit. We had many years of tree prunings on hand, but you can use piñon or almost any kind of wood available.

On the morning of the roast we lit the wood and kept adding to the fire until we had a good 5- to 6-inch layer of ashes covering the whole rock-lined pit. The goats were cut and quartered and basted heavily with store-bought barbecue sauce, as we didn't have any secret recipe. We wrapped the goats in heavy-duty aluminum foil and then covered them with heavy wet gunny sacks. We tied loops of wire to the ends of the gunny sacks to make removing them from the coals easier. We placed the meat carefully among the coals and covered it with more coals. We then placed smaller rocks over and around the meat and burned more wood in the pit to heat the rocks. We continued piling new coals over the meat until we had about as many on top as we did underneath. We covered it all lightly with dirt to keep the heat in.

After 6 hours, all the guests assembled to help. We carefully brushed the dirt away and lifted a gunny sack enough to let us test the meat. Perfect! The meat was tender and juicy and almost fell off the bone by itself. The fiesta was on!

THE BIG BARBECUE
(Pork, Beef, Goat)

Carlos Martínez, Chuck Pacheco, and J.M. Barker, all from New Mexico, became good friends in school in Quito, Ecuador, in 1974. Because they lead different lives, they decided that the only way they could be sure of seeing each other at least once a year was to have a barbecue. They have held it every year since, going back to the same pit each year.

They spit-roast the goat. Wire it securely so it won't slip. Hang it over glowing charcoal coals and turn frequently. Renew the coals as needed. The only problem with spit-roasting is that you are at the mercy of the weather. If it's a particularly chilly or windy day, your meat is going to take longer to cook, so judge accordingly.

No such problem arises with the friends' pit-roasted 350-pound hog, which has been quartered. The following recipe is the result of their years of trial and error. It can be used for beef or any other meat. Some 200 to 300 guests show up for the barbecue, and each one brings a dish to add to the feast—pinto beans, salads, casseroles, capirotada, homemade bread. Needless to say, there's plenty of beer and wine.

Pit preparation: Dig a pit approximately 6 feet deep by 4 feet square. Place rocks in bottom of pit and prepare a bonfire. (The friends prefer oak for coals and soaked applewood for smoked flavor.) Burn until there is a good layer of coals. Cover coals with pieces of sod. Place wrapped meat on coals. Cover with a piece of sheet metal to seal in the heat. Put another layer of coals on top and another layer of sod (see illustration). The 350-pound quartered hog takes about 18 hours of cooking—so allow enough time! For smaller animals, Carlos estimates 40 minutes per pound of meat.

Meat preparation:
1 quart vegetable oil
1 pint vinegar
1 pint lemon juice
10 chopped garlic cloves
½ box sage
1 box oregano
Some basil and thyme
4 large onions
12 whole garlic cloves (optional)

Mix oil, vinegar, lemon juice, chopped garlic, sage, oregano, basil, and thyme. Using a 4-inch paint brush, paint mixture on meat. If desired, make slits in meat and poke in additional whole garlic cloves. Cut onions in rings and spread around meat. Wrap meat securely in aluminum foil. Wrap again with clean wet burlap and fasten with baling wire. Put into pit as directed above.

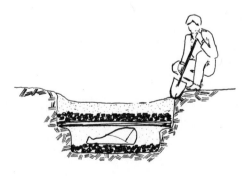

POULET MARENGO

For decades, whenever the talk has turned to restaurants in Santa Fe, the name always mentioned has been the **Pink Adobe**—and its equally famous owner, Rosalea Murphy. The combination of gourmet food, old Santa Fe ambience, and Rosalea's personal flair has made the restaurant justifiably famous. Try this dish and see why.

3 fresh fryers (2½-3 pounds each), split in half
1 cup flour
1 teaspoon salt
1 teaspoon paprika
2 tablespoons butter
2 tablespoons olive oil
1 wine glass Madeira
1 clove garlic, minced
bouquet garni
4-5 large mushrooms
12 pitted olives
1 small can whole onions
1 16-ounce can tomatoes
1 4-ounce can tomato juice
1 bay leaf
2 tablespoons flour
1 cup chicken broth

6 cooked shrimp, chopped
1 small can pâté de foie gras with truffles
18 small croutons

Put flour, salt, and paprika into a large paper bag. Shake chicken halves in this mixture one at a time until they are coated. In a heavy roaster, heat butter and oil and brown the halves one or two at a time. Add a little more oil if needed, but don't let the chicken get too greasy. When halves are nicely browned, drain off excess oil and start packing the roaster.

Place 3 halves on first layer, pressing them close together. Pour half the glass of wine on chickens. Distribute half the chopped garlic and a pinch of bouquet garni on each. Slice half the mushrooms over chickens, put 2 olives on each, and add half the drained onions. Squeeze half the can of tomatoes over all. Place the three remaining chicken halves on first layer and repeat with remaining seasonings, wine, mushrooms, olives, onions, and tomatoes. Pour can of tomato juice over all. Top with bay leaf. Cover roaster tightly with lid or foil. Bake at 325 degrees F for 2 hours (you might use less time at lower altitudes). Very carefully remove chickens to serving platter. They will be fork tender, so be careful. Keep in warm place while you make sauce.

With a wire whip, mix 2 tablespoons flour with the cup of chicken broth. Bring the juice in the roaster to a boil and beat in the broth till it thickens. If too thick, thin the sauce with a little Madeira.

Just before serving, spread the pâté on each chicken and sprinkle with shrimp and croutons. Serve the sauce separately. Serves 6.

QUICK CURRY

1 medium onion, chopped
½ cup diced celery
1 New Mexico apple, unpeeled, cored and diced
2 tablespoons vegetable oil
1 teaspoon chopped green chile
1 teaspoon minced crystalized ginger
2 cups diced cooked chicken, pork, beef, or lamb
1-3 teaspoons curry powder
¼ cup seedless raisins
1 cup evaporated milk
1 tablespoon cornstarch
salt and pepper to taste

In a large heavy skillet, saute the onion and celery until soft. Stir in the apple, chile, ginger, meat, curry powder, and raisins. Mix well and cover. Heat thoroughly. Mix cornstarch with a bit of the milk, then blend in with remaining milk. Heat thoroughly until mixture bubbles and thickens. Serve with rice. Serves 4.

ARROZ CON POLLO

This traditional Spanish recipe is one that Scottie King has adapted and serves often to her delighted guests. As Scottie points out, the dish can be prepared ahead of time, as it improves with standing. This amount serves 4, but the recipe can easily be doubled.

1 chicken or fowl, cut up as for frying
3 cups boiling water
1 large onion, chopped
1-2 cloves garlic, minced
1 cup raw rice, washed
¼ cup olive oil
1½ teaspoons salt
1 teaspoon paprika
½ teaspoon pepper
2 sprigs parsley, minced
1 bay leaf
½ teaspoon saffron
2-4 canned pimientos, chopped
oregano, basil, thyme (optional)

Put chicken in a large pot with boiling water and ½ teaspoon of the salt. Cover and simmer for 20-30 minutes (40-50 if it's a fowl). Meanwhile, mix onions, garlic, and rice. Heat olive oil in a large heavy skillet, add rice mixture, and stir until oil is well mixed in. Cover and fry VERY gently for 10 minutes. Stir frequently and take great care mixture does not brown. Add remaining salt, paprika, pepper, parsley, bay leaf, and saffron to chicken pot. Add such optional seasonings as you like, correct salt if need be, then spread rice mixture over the top of chicken. Cover and simmer gently until rice is soft and chicken is tender when pierced with a fork—from 40 to 60 minutes. Add the pimientos just before serving. Serves 4.

BEEF SATAY

Sometimes we forget that chile is popular all over the world. Here are two traditional Malaysian ways of using chile.

1 pound flank steak
1 small onion, minced
1 clove garlic, minced
1 teaspoon ground coriander
1 teaspoon cumin
1 teaspoon ginger
1 tablespoon chile powder
2 tablespoons oil
2 teaspoons soy sauce
2 teaspoons lemon juice

Cut steak in thin diagonal slices—"on the bias." Mix remaining ingredients together and pour over meat. Mix well and allow to marinate in the refrigerator overnight. Weave meat strips back and forth on metal skewers and broil under a hot flame (or on outdoor grill) until just cooked through, 5-8 minutes. Serve with Satay Sauce. Serves 4.

SATAY SAUCE FOR BEEF

1 small onion, minced
2 cloves garlic, minced
1 tablespoon oil
1 tablespoon soy sauce
1 cup water
2 tablespoons lemon juice
2 teaspoons sugar
⅓ cup crunchy peanut butter
2 teaspoons chile powder

Puree onion and garlic in food processor. Saute mixture in oil until soft. Add remaining ingredients and simmer gently until mixture is thick and smooth—about 6-8 minutes. Pour over Beef Satay.

PORK SATAY

2 pounds lean pork
2 tablespoons soy sauce
1 tablespoon minced fresh ginger
2 cloves garlic, minced
2 tablespoons peanut (or vegetable) oil
2 tablespoons white wine

⅓ cup crunchy peanut butter
1 tablespoon red chile powder
2 green onions, chopped
2 tablespoons lemon juice
1 cup water or white wine

Remove all visible fat from pork (pork loin or lean shoulder is good) and cut in cubes. Mix soy sauce, ginger, garlic, oil, and 2 tablespoons of white wine together and toss cubes in mixture until well coated. Leave to marinate for 30 minutes. Arrange cubes on metal skewers and broil, turning frequently and brushing with any remaining marinade, for 10 minutes or until cooked through. Meanwhile, heat peanut butter, chile powder, onion, lemon juice, and water or white wine together in a small saucepan and simmer gently until thickened. Serve pork with peanut sauce.

MANSION STEAK BÉARNAISE

The old Luna home in Los Lunas, south of Albuquerque, has been restored to its former elegance and is now a restaurant, known, naturally enough, as **Luna Mansion.** This is one of the specialties of the house.

4 steaks (rib, T-bone, or other)
1½ cups shredded crabmeat
¾ cup melted butter (not margarine)
3 egg yolks
1 tablespoon lemon juice
1 teaspoon tarragon
pinch seasoning salt
pinch paprika
drop Worcestershire sauce

Melt butter and set aside to cool. Take egg yolks at room temperature and whisk. In double boiler over hot (not boiling) water, add clarified butter (solids will have settled) to yolks, a tablespoon at a time, whisking after each addition. Add lemon juice and seasonings. Whisk. Sauce should be the consistency of thick gravy. Broil steaks to desired doneness, top with cold shredded crabmeat, and pour sauce over all. Serve immediately. Serves 4.

HOBBS BARBECUED RIBS

1 cup tomato sauce or puree
¼ cup honey
1 teaspoon cumin
2 tablespoons chile powder
¼ cup lemon juice
1 clove garlic, minced (optional)
1 tablespoon minced onion
salt to taste
3 pounds pork spareribs

Mix all ingredients except ribs. Spread on ribs and let stand for at least an hour. Grill over a slow fire (or in 325-degree oven)until they are tender, basting occasionally with sauce. If ribs haven't browned sufficiently by the time they are almost cooked, turn up the heat to finish them. Serves 3-4.

TRUDY'S BLEU-BURGERS

It takes a caring cook and a special touch to come up with a really good hamburger, and Trudy seems to be one of those cooks. **Trudy's Restaurant,** originally in Las Vegas and now in Raton, serves a pleasing mix of New Mexican and Italian dishes. The deceptively simple bleu-burger is on the menu.

1 pound lean (85%) ground chuck or round
1 Kaiser roll, warmed
1 ounce bleu cheese
1½ ounces cream cheese
1 tablespoon heavy cream

Make beef into one patty and grill to desired doneness. Meanwhile, mash bleu cheese and mix with cream cheese and cream in a small saucepan. Warm and stir over low heat, but do not allow to boil. When mixture is warmed through, spoon over the freshly grilled hamburger on the warm Kaiser roll. Serves 1.

SILVER CITY SAUSAGE

Sometimes the sausage meat you buy in a supermarket just doesn't seem worthwhile. But if you have a meat grinder or, better yet, that modern cook's magic machine, the food processor, you can make your own sausage in minutes. This is a spicy version, somewhat like chorizo.

2 pounds pork roast
1 pound pork fat
3 cloves garlic, minced
4 teaspoons chile molido
2 tablespoons vinegar
2 teaspoons salt
1 teaspoon oregano
½ teaspoon cumin
1 small onion, minced

Cut the meat and fat in chunks and grind or process. Mix all ingredients together thoroughly (you'll probably have to use your hands). Refrigerate. You may wrap the sausage well and freeze it, but don't try to keep it too long.

RAILROAD PIE

I don't know how this quick dish got its name, but I suspect it's because the Grants cook who submitted it lives near the main east-west railroad tracks. Or can it be because it is quick and easy?

1 pound sausage meat, plain or hot
1 large can sweet potatoes
¼ cup cream
½ teaspoon ginger
¼ cup dark brown sugar

Make sausage into flat patties and brown in skillet. Drain sweet potatoes, saving juice. Cut potatoes in slices and line a buttered pie pan. Mix juice, cream, and ginger together and pour over potatoes. Sprinkle with brown sugar. Arrange sausage patties on top. If there are drippings in pan, pour 1 or 2 tablespoonfuls over top of pie. Bake at 350 degrees F for 20-30 minutes.

THE CARLSBAD CASSEROLE

It's really hard to beat this dish for good down-home flavor.

1 pound sausage meat (regular or hot)
1 cup rice
1 onion, minced
1 clove garlic, minced
1 bell pepper, seeded and chopped
1 cup tomato juice
1½ cups chicken stock
1 teaspoon chile powder (optional)
salt and pepper to taste
½ teaspoon oregano

Break up sausage meat in skillet and brown lightly. Drain off excess fat. Mix in rice, onion, garlic, and pepper. Stir and cook over medium heat for 3 minutes. Mix in remaining ingredients and pour into covered baking dish. Bake at 350 degrees F for 40 minutes, stirring occasionally and adding hot water if rice becomes too dry. Serves 4.

HALLOWEEN HARVEST PUMPKIN

Mark and Deborah Nohl are avid gardeners, but, like the rest of us, they frequently end the season with a surplus of vegetables—and a forecast of frost. Confronted with a basketful of produce rescued from the garden one freezing night, Deborah had the answer. She dreamed up this most unusual stuffed pumpkin and had a party. Now her pumpkin has become a family tradition.

1 medium pumpkin
1 large onion, chopped
2 tablespoons vegetable oil
2-3 cloves garlic, minced
1 large Polish sausage or Mexican chorizo
assorted vegetables (see below)
½-1 pound cheddar cheese, grated

Preheat oven to 325 degrees F. Cut a lid out of pumpkin and set aside. Remove seeds and strings from pumpkin. Cook in oven without lid for 30 minutes. Meanwhile, saute onion in vegetable oil until transparent. Add garlic, then sausage, sliced or cubed. Drain off excess fat. Then add whatever vegetables you have from your garden: zucchini, tomatoes, green beans, snow peas, limas, crookneck squash, green chile, fresh corn, chayotes—take your pick. Saute lightly but do not cook. Layer this mixture in the pumpkin alternating with cheese. Place uncooked lid on pumpkin and bake until pumpkin is tender. When serving, make sure you scoop the delicious pumpkin meat from sides with each serving. Serve with jalapeño cornbread and hot apple cider. How many this serves depends on how large the pumpkin, how many vegetables you've filled it with, and how hungry your guests are.

LAMB AND MUTTON

New Mexico is sheep country and has been since the first Spanish explorers set foot on the *tierra encantada*. Navajos and Pueblos alike adopted the woolly newcomers and adapted their diets to the new meat. Lamb and mutton dishes—and goat too—therefore have long been popular on frontier and reservation. Later arrivals on the scene, the Scots and English, brought their broths and stews; the Greeks and Lebanese contributed their dishes. In *The Best from New Mexico Kitchens* we brought you some lamb and mutton favorites. Here are a few more.

ROAST LAMB WITH WHITE WINE

The late Helen Evans Brown became famous in the 1940s and '50s because in her many cookbooks and articles she introduced the cuisine of the West as something unique and delicious—much to the astonishment of Easterners who had always thought that all cooking began in Paris and ended in New York. This is Helen's recipe for roast lamb, one that has always been my favorite. The alcohol fumes have been known to pop open the oven door—but don't let that worry you! Enjoy the aroma, then shut the door again and continue roasting the lamb.

1 leg of lamb
12 cloves garlic
2 cups white wine (Riesling, Moselle, white burgundy, etc.)
2 cups sliced pitted ripe olives

Put the peeled cloves of garlic in the roasting pan with the leg of lamb. Pour over the white wine, jab the meat well with an ice pick, and baste at least a dozen times during the cooking. The garlic thickens the sauce and perfumes the lamb, but, oddly, doesn't overpower it. Roast using your favorite method. (I prefer 400 degrees F for 5 minutes, then 325 degrees F for the rest of the time needed, which will be about 10 minutes per pound.) Just before serving, heat the olives in the sauce and serve with the roast.

LEMON LAMB CHOPS

There's nothing like lemon for bringing out the best in lamb.

8 loin lamb chops
½ cup lemon juice
½ teaspoon grated lemon rind
¼ teaspoon garlic powder or 1 crushed clove garlic
salt and pepper to taste

Spread chops in shallow glass dish. Mix lemon juice, rind, and garlic and drizzle over chops. Marinate for an hour, turning chops occasionally. Broil (but please don't overcook them), season with salt and pepper, and serve to 4.

PEASANT LAMB

Albuquerque's Greek community will recognize this traditional country-style casserole. It has the attributes of being easy—and absolutely delicious.

2 pounds lean shoulder of lamb, cut in cubes
1 pound feta cheese
2 pounds fresh tomatoes
salt and pepper
1 tablespoon lemon juice
2 tablespoons olive oil

Remove excess fat from meat and put cubes in a baking dish. Cut the cheese in small cubes and scatter over the meat. Peel and slice the tomatoes and arrange over cheese. Sprinkle with salt and pepper, lemon juice, and olive oil. Bake uncovered at 350 degrees F for about 1½ hours, basting frequently. Serves 6.

LEBANESE LAMB TARTS

These delectable little lamb tarts are adapted from a traditional Lebanese recipe.

3 tablespoons butter
½ cup piñon nuts or imported pine nuts
1 pound lean lamb, ground
2 medium onions, minced
1 teaspoon salt
¼ teaspoon pepper
¼ teaspoon pumpkin pie spice mixture
pastry for tart shells (filo or your own)

Heat butter in pan and lightly saute piñon nuts. Set aside nuts. Add meat to pan and fry, breaking up thoroughly. Before it browns, add the onions, salt, pepper, and spice. Mix thoroughly. Cover and simmer gently until meat is cooked and tender—about 20 minutes. Remove from heat and mix in piñon nuts. Cool. Fill tiny tart shells with mixture and bake at 400 degrees F until pastry is crisp and meat has been heated and browned. How long this will take will depend on the size of your tart shells. You'll probably have very tiny ones for a stand-around cocktail party or medium size ones for a luncheon.

SHEPHERD'S PIE

The early settlers were good hands at turning leftovers into like-new meals, and those who struggled through the Depression in New Mexico also knew their way around a pound of hamburger or a bit of yesterday's pot roast. So maybe it's time to remind ourselves of two of their born-again casseroles.

2 cups leftover mashed potatoes
¼ cup warm milk
1 egg
salt and pepper to taste
2 cups finely chopped leftover meat
1 medium onion, chopped
¼ cup minced parsley
½ cup finely chopped celery, including tops
1 cup leftover gravy
   or 1 cup mushroom soup
   or ½ cup stock, ½ cup sour cream
½ cup sliced mushrooms (optional)
½ cup sliced cooked carrots (optional)
½ cup grated cheddar cheese

Beat the egg and milk into mashed potatoes and season as necessary. Heat meat, onion, parsley, and celery in leftover gravy and allow to simmer gently for a minute or 2. As you can see, what you make of this recipe depends on what you have left in the fridge. With leftover lamb, the mushroom soup and mushrooms are a good combination. With leftover beef, a dash of Worcestershire sauce helps the seasoning along. If you have dibs and dabs of vegetables, toss them in. If the mixture is too thick, thin with stock or wine or whatever. Turn the meat mixture into a casserole and spread mashed potatoes over the top like a crust. Sprinkle with cheese and bake at 375 degrees F until heated through and golden brown.

TAMALE PIE

This particular version is the specialty of a young Gallup girl who adapted it from an aunt's recipe.

1½ cups leftover meat, chopped
1 cup leftover gravy
1 cup red chile sauce
1 small onion, chopped
1 can niblet corn, drained
salt and pepper to taste
garlic powder (optional)

3 cups water or stock
¾ cup yellow cornmeal
salt to taste

Heat meat with gravy, chile sauce, onion, and corn and season to taste. Meanwhile boil stock or water and stir in cornmeal. Cook, stirring over low heat until mush is thick. Turn meat mixture into casserole and top with spoonfuls of cornmeal mush evenly distributed over surface. Bake at 350 degrees F for about 40 minutes.

SALAMI

And from Rosalie Howland comes this unusual do-it-yourself recipe.

2¼ pounds lean ground beef
¼ teaspoon salt
¼-½ teaspoon garlic powder
½ teaspoon cracked pepper
1 tablespoon liquid smoke
1 tablespoon mustard seed
2 tablespoons Morton's Tender Quick Salt (no substitute!)
¾ cup water

Mix all ingredients together well. Shape into rolls about 2½ inches in diameter, no larger. Wrap each roll in 2 sheets of aluminum foil, shiny side against meat. Twist ends of each sheet separately. Refrigerate rolls for 24 hours. Poke 4 or 5 holes along bottoms of rolls or open one end of each roll (for draining drippings). Set rolls on racks in pans and place in 350-degree F oven. Slightly tilt pans (use another small pan or a couple of pieces of crumpled foil) to allow fat to drain thoroughly. Bake for 1 to 1¼ hours. Cool and rewrap in fresh foil. Ready to serve or freeze.

GAME AND FISH

These words of wisdom come from John Crenshaw, the popular and knowledgeable editor of *New Mexico Wildlife:*

Big game meat should be a treat, as it's usually acquired against high odds at considerable investment in time, money, and physical effort. It's lower in saturated fats and higher in proteins and minerals than comparable cuts of choice beef, and its excellent flavor is its own. It deserves respect both in the field and in the kitchen.

Unfortunately, poor field care has ruined tons of meat and ruined untold appetites, to the point that many cooks approach wild meat overcautiously, marinating it too long, spicing it too heavily, and cooking it until it's dry and tough.

Although some quite experienced hunters may argue some of the following points, especially that on skinning, we have consistently enjoyed excellent meat by employing them, even keeping meat fresh and clean on a dry, dusty antelope hunt when temperatures soared above 100 degrees F.

Briefly: Tag the animal according to the game codes; completely eviscerate it, being sure not to leave the wind-and food pipes in the neck. Hang it, if possible, and *skin it immediately* (on the ground, if necessary, keeping the hide stretched out to protect the meat from dirt). Handle the skin from the flesh side to avoid getting hair on the carcass. Thoroughly pepper the carcass, especially where cuts have been made in between the hams, in the abdomen, on the neck, etc., to repel flies. Let the carcass hang until it's no longer sticky to the touch, then place it in game bags and keep them hung in the coolest, airiest place available. Bags should be about the weave of muslin, tightly woven enough to keep out dirt, pine needles, and such, but loose enough to allow air to circulate.

If necessary for transport, bone the meat right there, using plastic leaf bags as a work area, then carry the meat on a packframe (protected, again, in the meat sacks). At home, cut away fat and gristle (add beef suet to deerburger) and bone the meat if that remains to be done. Double-wrap it tightly to seal out air and deep-freeze in coldest part of freezer.

Fish, too, require immediate tending. They should be kept alive either in a live well or fish basket until it's time to clean them, or they should be stunned, eviscerated, and iced immediately.

Birds should be drawn, then plucked or skinned, and iced as quickly as possible—particularly those such as doves, quail, or other upland game likely to be taken during warm weather.

In all cases, moisture, dirt, heat, and hair (or feathers) can contaminate the meat. Consider the investment and the possible return: the first is high, the second can match it.

CHICKAREE SQUIRRELS

Two hunting partners, Joe Pierce and Vern Wolgamott, like to cook their squirrels this way.

4-8 chickaree (pine) squirrels
2 tablespoons shortening
flour for dredging
1 large onion, chopped
1-2 cans beer (any brand)
2-4 green chiles, chopped
4 medium tomatoes, quartered
1 clove garlic, minced
salt and pepper to taste

Cut squirrels in quarters and soak several hours in salt water. Drain and rinse. Pat dry with paper towels. Melt shortening in a heavy skillet. Dredge meat in flour. Brown the meat and onion, adding more shortening if necessary. Add remaining ingredients, using just enough beer to cover the mixture. Cover skillet, simmer gently for 2 hours, adding beer as needed. Adjust seasoning. Serve over rice.

BROILED DOVE

Jack Herring, who is with the Game Management Division of the Department of Game and Fish, says this is the tastiest way to prepare doves.

**3-5 plucked (not skinned) dove breasts per person
thin-sliced bacon**

Wrap each dove breast in one layer (usually ½ slice) bacon, pinning it with a wooden toothpick. Broil, turning so all sides are done. When the bacon is crisp—usually 40 minutes—the doves are ready.

SWEET AND SOUR VENISON

Donna Herring recommends this recipe for the tougher cuts of your animal.

**2 pounds cubed venison (elk, deer, or antelope)
2 tablespoons vegetable oil
2 8-ounce cans tomato sauce
1½ teaspoons red chile powder
¼ teaspoon ground cumin
⅛ teaspoon garlic powder
2 teaspoons paprika
¼ cup dark brown sugar
½ cup red wine vinegar
2 cups sliced carrots
2 small onions, chopped
1 large bell pepper, chopped**

Brown meat in oil. Combine with other ingredients and heat through. Transfer to a slow cooker (crock pot) and simmer for 8-10 hours on low setting. Or cover tightly and simmer very gently on stove top for 2 or 3 hours or until meat is tender. Serve over rice or macaroni. Serves 6-8.

ELK ROAST

This is the way Molly Crenshaw prepares elk as a pot roast.

3-5 pound elk roast
3 tablespoons shortening
1 medium can cream of mushroom soup
1 package instant onion soup

Melt shortening in a dutch oven and brown the roast on all sides. Mix onion soup and mushroom soup and add. Cover tightly and simmer very gently until roast is done to your taste. If gravy becomes too dry during cooking, add a little water or red wine.

HARVEST

The simplest way is often the best way—and here's John Crenshaw's recipe to prove it.

boned deer chops (2-3 per person), sliced 1 inch thick
vegetable oil or butter
salt and pepper to taste

Trim fat and gristle from meat. Salt and pepper very lightly. Saute chops in oil or butter, turning them occasionally. Cook to taste—just pinkish in the center is recommended—but do not allow meat to become dry and tough through overcooking. To make a real ranch meal, serve this with hot cornbread and pinto beans, raw onion on the side, and fresh summer squash dipped in egg-and-milk batter, rolled in cornmeal, and fried in butter. A fresh garden salad and a pitcher of cold milk make this meal just tops.

QUAIL IN WHITE WINE

Joel Roth, an attorney in Santa Fe, contributed this most elegant quail recipe to *New Mexico Wildlife*.

8 quail
½ cup butter
2 shallots, chopped
2 cloves garlic, minced
4 cloves, broken
dash of coarse-cracked peppercorns
2 cups full-bodied dry white wine
1 bay leaf
4 tablespoons butter
4 tablespoons flour
salt and pepper to taste
chopped chives (optional)

Melt ½ cup butter in an enamel saucepan large enough to hold the quail and brown the shallots, garlic, cloves, and peppercorns for about 8 minutes, stirring constantly. Do not allow butter to burn. Saute quail in butter and spices until well browned, then add wine and bay leaf. Simmer quail for 30 minutes, uncovered. Remove quail and set aside. Strain and reserve sauce. Make a roux by melting 4 tablespoons butter in the large pan and blending in flour. Stir in the sauce and cook, stirring, until it is thick. Add salt and pepper to taste and chives if desired. Return quail to sauce, cover, and heat through. Place quail on warm plates and cover with sauce. Serves 4.

FRIED QUAIL

Irene Crenshaw of Raton agrees with her son John that sometimes the simplest ways of cooking game are the best.

2-3 quail per person
flour
butter or vegetable shortening
salt and pepper to taste

Lightly dust quail with flour. Melt shortening in a heavy skillet and brown the birds. Add salt and pepper, turn down heat, cover skillet, and gently cook until birds are done, turning them occasionally.

MALLARD DINNER

Here's another very simple old-fashioned method that emphasizes the intrinsic flavor of the ducks, with no embellishments. No stuffing, no extras. Ducks done this way, although well cooked, should not be hard or dry.

2 ducks
salt and pepper

Ducks should be dressed, then aged from 3 to 5 days without freezing. Set oven at 450 degrees F. Place whole ducks, breast side up, in a big covered roasting pan. Season with salt and pepper. Put about 1 inch of hot water in the pan. Cover tightly and roast for about 15 minutes. Turn down oven to 350 degrees F and continue roasting for 45 more minutes, basting every 15 minutes with pan liquid. If ducks are not young, you may have to add up to an hour more cooking and basting time. Serves 4.

CAPIROTADA

Everyone in New Mexico seems to have a favorite version of this popular dessert that is also called sopa.

1½ cups brown sugar
1½ cups water
1 3-inch stick of cinnamon
1 whole clove
2 tablespoons butter
6-8 slices leftover pound cake or Indian bread
½ pound jack or longhorn cheese, grated
1 cup seedless raisins
1 cup chopped Valencia—no skins—peanuts (optional)
2 ounces brandy (optional)

Boil sugar and water together with cinnamon stick and clove until mixture becomes syrupy—about 15 minutes. Stir in butter. Lightly toast the pound cake or Indian bread (any bread will do, but homemade would be best). Cube the bread and spread a layer in a buttered casserole. Add layers of cheese, raisins and peanuts. Repeat until ingredients are used up. Remove cinnamon and clove with slotted spoon from syrup. Stir brandy into syrup and pour over all ingredients. Bake at 350 degrees F for about 30 minutes.

MARMALADE SOUFFLE

The perfect ending for a New Mexico meal of enchiladas, tacos, and tamales. Use the best and fruitiest marmalade you can, follow directions explicitly, and you'll have a perfect souffle every time.

4 egg whites
4 tablespoons confectioners' sugar
4 tablespoons orange marmalade

Beat egg whites stiff. Gradually beat in sugar, a spoonful at a time. Fold in marmalade. Turn into a well-buttered double boiler top. Cover tightly, set over simmering water and steam for 50 minutes. DO NOT LIFT LID AND PEEK! If water runs low, quickly add a bit more boiling water in bottom. Serves 4. Serve with Brandy Sauce.

BRANDY SAUCE

1 egg yolk
1 tablespoon brandy
½ cup confectioners' sugar

Beat egg yolk, brandy, and sugar together. If mixture is too thick for your taste, add a little more brandy. Serve over Marmalade Souffle.

INDIAN PUDDING

This traditional dessert probably sneaked into New Mexico from New England. Dare we think that it came here with the famous LaFarge family from Rhode Island? In Rhode Island, it would have been made with stone-ground *white* cornmeal. Elsewhere, yellow is more commonly used. Either way, it's a fantastic treat for a cold winter's night.

6 cups milk
½ cup cornmeal
⅓ cup brown sugar
2 tablespoons molasses
2 teaspoons cinnamon
½ teaspoon ginger
¼ teaspoon nutmeg
2 tablespoons butter
1 cup heavy cream

Heat milk to simmering point and stir in all ingredients except cream. Simmer for 5 minutes, stirring constantly, until mixture is smooth. Pour into baking dish and bake at 325 degrees F for an hour, stirring occasionally. Take out, stir in the cream, return to oven, and bake 30 minutes longer. Serve hot with ice-cold heavy cream or vanilla ice cream. This amount should serve 10, but I've seen it disappear into only 5 persons.

CREAMY BLINTZES

Among the earliest arrivals in New Mexico over the Santa Fe Trail were a number of German Jews. They stayed on to found families, businesses, dynasties. Many became associated with Indian pueblos and, through their mercantile operations, helped to open the roads to travel, trade, and understanding. Here, then, a traditional Jewish dish.

basic crêpe recipe (see page 48)
½ cup cottage cheese
1 large package (13-ounce) cream cheese
1 egg
1 teaspoon vanilla
¼ teaspoon cinnamon
¼ cup chopped seedless raisins
3 tablespoons butter or margarine
cherry or plum jam
sour cream

Prepare crêpes as directed, cooking on one side only. Stack with waxed paper between crêpes. Put cottage cheese in blender or food processor and blend smooth. Or push through a sieve. Blend in cream cheese, egg, vanilla, and cinnamon. Mix in raisins. Spoon a tablespoonful or two in the center of cooked side of each crêpe. Fold up into little packages. Saute in part of the butter in a large skillet. Cook until golden brown on each side, about 4 minutes, adding more butter as needed. Serve warm with sour cream and jam or confectioners' sugar.

FROZEN CHOCOLATE MOUSSE CAKE

Here's something very rich and special from an Alamogordo cook.

1 large bag (13-14 ounces) chocolate chips
½ cup butter
2 ounces unsweetened chocolate
1 teaspoon instant coffee
4 large eggs
1 tablespoon sugar
1 teaspoon vanilla
1 tablespoon flour

Melt chocolate chips, butter, and unsweetened chocolate with instant coffee in top of double boiler. Combine eggs and sugar in another pan set over hot water and beat until sugar is dissolved and mixture barely warm. Remove from stove, add vanilla, and beat with electric mixer on high speed until very thick and double in volume. Fold in flour. Put a little of egg mixture into chocolate mixture, then fold chocolate into remaining egg mixture. Turn into ungreased 8-inch square pan. Bake at 375 degrees F for 15-20 minutes. Cake should be soft in center but crusty on top. Cool in tin, cover with foil, and freeze. Remove from freezer 2-3 hours before serving. To serve, cut in squares and top with whipped cream. Set pan in hot water for a few seconds for easy removal of mousse.

WIZARD CHOCOLATE MOUSSE

2 cups commercial sour cream
½ cup sugar
½ cup crumbled macaroons
3 ounces unsweetened chocolate, melted
1 tablespoon rum or brandy
1 teaspoon vanilla

Mix all ingredients together thoroughly. Spoon into a freezer tray and freeze until firm but not rock hard. About 3 hours should do it. Scoop into glasses and sprinkle with chocolate shot or shaved sweet chocolate. Serves 4.

PEANUT BRITTLE MOUSSE

Let's hope you've made your very own peanut brittle with Portales-grown skinless Valencia peanuts! (See page 111.)

½ pound peanut brittle
2 cups heavy cream
1 teaspoon vanilla
½ cup roasted Valencia peanuts, chopped

Grind up the peanut brittle in your processor or put it in a paper bag and pound it with a mallet. Whip the cream and vanilla. Fold in powdered brittle. Freeze in ice cube tray, or, better yet, in an ice cream freezer. Garnish each serving with chopped peanuts.

CHRISTINA'S ALWAYS-PERFECT FLAN

Back by popular demand—this recipe was first published in *The Best from New Mexico Kitchens* and has now become a classic. You get a perfect flan every time, even at high altitudes, where bubbles in the custard can be a problem.

½ cup sugar
8 egg yolks
2 egg whites
1 14-ounce can sweetened condensed milk
1 13-ounce can evaporated milk
2 cups whole milk or water
1 teaspoon vanilla

In a heavy skillet, melt sugar, stirring constantly. When it is light brown, pour it into a 2-quart mold. Tip mold quickly in all directions so that caramel coats the inside. (It will get very hot, so hold it with tongs.) Set mold aside. Beat eggs until thick. Beat in condensed milk, evaporated milk, whole milk (or water), and vanilla. Pour into prepared mold. Cover securely with a tight lid or with 3 layers of foil tied down. Place on rack in pressure cooker with 2-3 cups of water (follow manufacturer's directions) and cook for 20 minutes after pressure comes up. (It will take a bit longer at higher altitudes.) Cool rapidly. After custard is chilled, turn out on a serving dish. Serves 12.

RUIDOSO GOLD ICE CREAM

Time to get out your ice cream freezer—this one is worth the effort.

8 ounces dried apricots
2-inch strip of lemon rind
1 tablespoon lemon juice
¼ cup Grand Marnier or brandy
4 egg yolks
¾ cup sugar
1 cup half-and-half
1 cup heavy cream

Put apricots and lemon peel in saucepan, cover with cold water, and bring to a boil. Simmer until apricots are tender. Some take longer than others. Drain, discard lemon rind, and sieve or process apricots into a puree. Add lemon juice and Grand Marnier. Beat egg yolks and sugar together until light and thick. Heat half-and-half (but don't boil). Pour gradually into egg mixture, beating constantly. Return mixture to saucepan and cook over low heat, beating or stirring constantly, until slightly thickened. Remove from heat, stir in apricot mixture, and cool. Whip cream and fold in. Turn into freezer cannister and freeze according to manufacturer's instructions.

OLD-TIME BOILED CUSTARD

Luke Lyon of Los Alamos contributes this old family recipe.

1 gallon milk, heated almost to boiling
2 cups sugar
12 egg yolks, beaten
¼ teaspoon salt
12 egg whites, beaten stiff
2 tablespoons vanilla
whipped cream
nutmeg

Add sugar to hot milk. Pour ½ cup of the milk into the egg yolks, then add to milk mixture. Stir and cook for 5 minutes (very gently). Cool. Stir in vanilla and fold in beaten egg whites. Serve cold topped with whipped cream and sprinkled with nutmeg. Family black sheep have been known to add spirits. [Luke doesn't say, but this looks as if it could serve 16 people easily.—SMC.]

MUD PIE

The historic **Luna Mansion** in Los Lunas, south of Albuquerque, is now an elegant restaurant, where this lovely pie is served up to eager guests.

1½ cups crushed chocolate wafers
½ cup butter, melted
1 quart coffee ice cream, softened
12 ounces fudge topping
¼ cup slivered almonds
1 cup heavy cream, whipped

Mix crushed cookies and melted butter in 9-inch pie pan. Press to form crust. Cool. Press ice cream into crust. Freeze until hardened. Spread fudge topping over ice cream. Sprinkle with slivered almonds. Serve topped with whipped cream.

INCREDIBLE PIE

Super easy and super delicious—that's this secret recipe shared with us by a Roswell hostess.

4 medium eggs
1 14-ounce can evaporated milk
¼ cup rum or water
⅓ cup flour
⅔ cup sugar
1 teaspoon vanilla
1 cup flaked coconut
½ cup butter
nutmeg

Butter a 9-inch pie pan and dust lightly with flour. Set oven at 325 degrees F. Put all ingredients except nutmeg in a blender or processor and blend smooth. Pour into a pie pan and sprinkle with nutmeg. Bake for 45 minutes or until custard sets. Cool before serving. The pie will form its own crust as it bakes. [I've tried this recipe using 1 cup of blanched almonds instead of the coconut and ¼ teaspoon of almond extract instead of the vanilla. It makes a quite different pie with a marzipan-y taste and texture.—SMC]

PUMPKIN PRALINE PIE

The old Loretto Convent in Bernalillo has become a popular restaurant, **La Hacienda de Baca.** This dessert is one of their most popular.

1¼ cups plus 1 tablespoon flour
½ teaspoon salt
⅓ cup vegetable oil
2 tablespoons cold water

⅓ cup chopped pecans
1 cup brown sugar
2 tablespoons melted margarine

2 eggs
1 cup minus 2 tablespoons pumpkin (cooked or canned)
⅔ cup brown sugar
1 tablespoon flour
¼ teaspoon ground cloves
⅛ teaspoon mace
½ teaspoon cinnamon
½ teaspoon ginger
½ teaspoon salt
1 cup half-and-half
whipping cream
pecan halves

Crust: Sift flour with salt, add vegetable oil, and mix well with fork. Add cold water and mix. Shape into ball and roll out between 2 sheets of waxed paper. Shape into 9-inch pie pan and refrigerate for 1 hour. *Praline:* Mix well chopped pecans, brown sugar, and margarine. Spread evenly over bottom of pie crust. *Filling:* Beat 2 eggs well. Add remaining ingredients and mix until just blended. Pour over pecan mixture. Bake 50 minutes at 375 degrees F. Cool. Serve topped with whipped cream and pecan half.

DENNIS'S CARAMEL PIE

1 8-inch baked pie shell
1 14-ounce can sweetened condensed milk
½ cup shelled toasted piñon nuts
1 cup whipping cream

Note: It is important to follow directions exactly. Put the unopened can of condensed milk in a pot of water to cover. The water MUST cover the can at all times. Bring to boil.

Simmer gently for 1 hour and 20 minutes. (This may take longer at high altitudes.) Leave can in water to cool for at least ½ hour. Then, very carefully, cover can with a damp clean cloth as you open it. (Otherwise the warm caramel can squirt out and possibly burn you.) Spread caramel in pie shell and sprinkle with chopped piñon nuts. Chill. Whip the cream and spread over pie. This makes a very sweet, gooey pie with the kind of flavor popular in Mexico and South America.

EMPANADITAS

Depending on what you put inside these little turnovers, they can be used as appetizer, cocktail party snack, or dessert. They can be baked—as they are in this version—or they can be deep fried, in which case you'll want to use a not-too-short regular pastry recipe.

2 3-ounce packages cream cheese
1 cup butter
2 cups flour

Cream the butter and cheese together until well blended. Add the flour and work into a ball. Chill overnight. Roll out on lightly floured board and cut into 3- or 4-inch circles. Put a spoonful of filling on one half of the pastry, dampen edges, fold over, and seal by pressing around edges with a fork. Bake at 375 degrees F for 15-20 minutes or until golden brown. *Fillings:* Try using applesauce and cinnamon; homemade or bottled mincemeat; pumpkin or sweet potato puree and brown sugar; slivers of jack cheese and quince paste; jam; brown sugar and cinnamon; grated sweet chocolate; refried beans and cheese; minced leftover chicken or turkey with green chile and onion; minced leftover pork or beef seasoned with chile and dampened with gravy...well, the list is endless!

FARMINGTON FANCY

Here's a treat made with those good New Mexico apples.

4 cups thinly sliced tart apples
½ cup red currant jelly
1 teaspoon lemon juice
½ cup whole wheat flour
½ cup brown sugar
1 teaspoon cinnamon
¼ cup butter
½ cup chopped pecans

Arrange apples in deep buttered 9-inch pie pan. Heat currant jelly and lemon juice, stirring, until melted. Drizzle evenly over apples. Mix flour, sugar, and cinnamon together and cut in butter until mixture is crumbly. Mix in pecans. Sprinkle evenly over apples. Bake at 350 degrees F for about 30 minutes. Serve warm with cream.

MARLBOROUGH PIE

1 9-inch unbaked pie shell
2 cups tart applesauce
3 tablespoons butter, melted
1 cup sugar
3 tablespoons lemon juice
1 teaspoon grated lemon rind
4 eggs, slightly beaten

Combine all ingredients and mix well. Pour into pie shell and bake at 450 degrees F for 15 minutes, then 275 degrees F for about 1 hour longer. Filling should be golden brown and cut like firm jelly.

PINK ADOBE FRENCH APPLE PIE

And here it is, that famous French Apple Pie. Rosalea of the **Pink Adobe** says she has no idea how many she's made over the years. "Thousands, hundreds of thousands, maybe millions." Forget about calories when you eat this concoction.

2 cups flour
¾ cup lard
1 teaspoon salt
cold water

1 pound apples
½ teaspoon nutmeg
½ teaspoon cinnamon
2 tablespoons lemon juice
¼ cup seedless raisins
½ cup sugar
1 cup brown sugar
2 tablespoons flour
½ cup (¼ pound) butter
½ cup chopped pecans
¼ cup milk

Work flour, lard, and salt together until crumbly. Add 6 or 7 tablespoons cold water until dough holds together. Form into 2 balls. Roll out to line and top a 9-inch pie pan. *Filling:* Wash, peel, core, and slice apples into pie shell. Sprinkle with lemon juice, nutmeg, and cinnamon. Spread with raisins and white sugar. Mix brown sugar, flour, and butter. Spread over contents. Sprinkle with pecans and most of milk. Cover with pastry, prick with fork, and brush with remaining bit of milk. Bake at 450 degrees F for 10 minutes. Reduce heat to 350 degrees F and bake for another 30 minutes. Serve hot with Hard Sauce.

HARD SAUCE

½ cup butter
1½ cup confectioners' or powdered sugar
1 tablespoon boiling water
1 teaspoon brandy or rum

Cream the butter until light. Beat in the sugar and add 1 tablespoon boiling water. Then beat in brandy. Serve with French Apple Pie.

WELCOME APPLE PIE

This unusual apple pie is halfway between the traditional all-American favorite and an old-time Marlborough pie. Sylvia Norred, who is a tourist counselor at the Glen Rio Welcome Center on the northeast New Mexico border with Texas, makes this with golden delicious apples. But almost any good New Mexico apple would work well.

1 10-inch pie shell, unbaked
1½ cups sugar
3 tablespoons flour
2 eggs, beaten
½ cup melted margarine
½ teaspoon cinnamon
½ teaspoon nutmeg
1 teaspoon vanilla
3 cups peeled, cored, and chopped apples

Mix sugar and flour. Add eggs, margarine, nutmeg, cinnamon, and vanilla. Blend well. Stir in chopped apples. Pour into pie shell. Bake at 425 degrees F for 15 minutes, then 350 degrees F for 30 minutes or until done. Cool and serve with whipped cream, if desired.

LINCOLN COUNTY CIDER PIE

We like to think that this old-time recipe arrived in southern New Mexico with the first Scots and English ranchers, back in the middle of the 19th century.

1½ cups flour
2 tablespoons sugar
⅓ cup butter
1 egg yolk
1 tablespoon lemon juice

¾ pound tart green apples
1 cup dry alcoholic cider
2 eggs
⅓ cup sugar
2 tablespoons flour

Pastry: Mix flour and sugar. Cut in butter till mixture is crumbly. Mix in egg and lemon juice to make a pastry. If more moisture is needed, add more lemon juice. Chill for 30 minutes. Roll out between sheets of waxed paper and fit into a deep 10- or 12-inch pie pan or flan tin. Butter a sheet of foil and press on top of pastry. Bake at 375 degrees F for 15 minutes. Remove foil and bake shell for 5-8 minutes longer or until pale gold. *Filling:* Peel and core apples (pippins or Granny Smiths are good) and slice in thick rounds. Cover with the cider and simmer until just barely tender. Remove apples with slotted spoon and let cool. Let cider cool, too. Beat eggs with sugar and flour until mixture is quite thick. Mix in the cooled cider and return to a large saucepan. Cook over low heat, beating constantly, until mixture comes to a boil and thickens. Remove from heat. Carefully arrange apples in pastry shell. Pour cider mixture over the top. Bake for 18 minutes or until set on top. Serve warm with Cider Syllabub.

CIDER SYLLABUB

This creamy sauce is served ice cold, poured over warm Lincoln County Cider Pie. Oh, yum!

¾ cup dry alcoholic apple cider
½ cup confectioners' sugar
3 tablespoons lemon juice
grated rind 1 lemon
1 cup heavy cream
1 tablespoon brandy

Mix cider with sugar, lemon juice, and lemon rind. Whip the cream until it holds stiff peaks. Gradually beat in cider mixture and brandy. (Sauce will thin down to pouring consistency.) Pour into a pitcher, cover, and refrigerate overnight before using.

ROYAL NEW MEXICO CHEESECAKE

1½ cups vanilla or chocolate wafer crumbs
3 tablespoons brown sugar
6 tablespoons butter
1½ pounds cream cheese
1 14-ounce can condensed milk
4 eggs, separated
1 cup sour cream
2 teaspoons grated lemon rind
1 tablespoon lemon juice

Lightly grease a 10-inch springform pan and set oven at 325 degrees F. Mash cookies into crumbs by placing them in a paper bag and rolling with a rolling pin, or by running them in a processor. Melt the butter over low heat and mix in crumbs and brown sugar. Press crumbs into the bottom and sides of the springform pan. Beat cream cheese and condensed milk together until blended. Beat in egg yolks one at a time, then sour cream, rind, and juice. Beat egg whites stiff and fold gently into cheese mixture. Pour into prepared pan and bake for 1¼ hours. Turn off oven and leave cheesecake in oven with door shut until cool. Refrigerate.

CARAMEL POUND CAKE

Edna Turner makes this delectable golden-brown pound cake to have on hand for unexpected company or as a treat when her grandchildren pop in. You'll want to reduce the baking powder at higher altitudes—Edna uses just ½ teaspoon at Santa Fe's 7,000-foot altitude, for example.

1½ cups butter
1 cup brown sugar
½ cup liquid brown sugar
¼ cup granulated sugar
5 eggs
1 tablespoon vanilla
3 cups sifted flour
1 teaspoon baking powder
¼ teaspoon salt
½ cup half-and-half
1 cup chopped pecans

If you can't find liquid brown sugar, substitute ½ cup of golden cane syrup and ¼ cup cold strong coffee and eliminate the granulated white sugar. Preheat oven to 350 degrees F. Grease and flour an angel food pan or a Bundt pan. Cream butter and sugars. Beat in eggs one at a time. Mix in vanilla. Sift flour, baking powder, and salt and add alternately with half-and-half, saving the last ½ cup of flour to mix with nuts before folding them into the mixture. Pour into prepared pan and bake for one hour. Remove from oven and set in pan of cold water until cool. Invert onto cake rack and dust with confectioners' sugar or frost with your favorite frosting.

MAURINE'S GINGERBREAD

We've tried them all, but we've never found a gingerbread with the flavor of this one. It's dark and moist, and its only drawback is that you'll eat too much of it.

1½ cups brown sugar
3 eggs
1 cup dark molasses
1 cup vegetable oil
3 cups flour
¼ teaspoon salt
1 teaspoon cinnamon
¼ teaspoon nutmeg
¼ teaspoon allspice
1 teaspoon baking soda
dash of white pepper
2 teaspoons ginger
1¼ cups boiling water

Set oven at 350 degrees F. Grease and flour a 9- x 15-inch baking pan. Combine brown sugar, eggs, molasses and oil. Sift in dry ingredients. Blend with spoon. Last, quickly stir in the water. Mix well and turn into pan. Bake for 45-50 minutes, or until center is just done. Don't overbake. Serve warm or cold. Cut in squares and top with whipped cream sprinkled with chopped candied ginger, if you want to be elegant. Or with vanilla ice cream. Or hot with a blob of real butter on top. Or cream cheese. Or....

TOASTED BUTTER PECAN CAKE

From the enormous pecan groves of Stahmann Farms, near Las Cruces, comes this doubly pecan-ful cake.

2 cups chopped Del Cerro pecans from New Mexico
1¼ cups butter
3 cups flour
½ teaspoon salt
2 teaspoons baking powder
2 cups sugar
5 eggs
1 cup milk
2 teaspoons vanilla

Toast the chopped pecans in ¼ cup of the butter in 350-degree F oven for 20-25 minutes. Stir occasionally and don't allow to burn. Cool. Sift flour, salt, and baking powder. Cream remaining cup of butter with sugar. Beat in eggs one at a time. Add dry ingredients alternately with milk. Stir in vanilla and 1 ⅓ cups of the nuts. Turn into 3 greased and floured 10-inch cake pans or 4 8-inch pans. Bake at 350 degrees F for 30 minutes for the 10-inch pans. Don't overbake. Cool slightly, then turn onto wire racks. When cake is cold, put layers together with Pecan Icing.

PECAN ICING

⅔ cup toasted pecans (from previous recipe)
2 large eggs
4 cups confectioners' sugar
⅔ cup butter, softened
2 teaspoons vanilla

Beat eggs, sugar, butter, and vanilla together until light and fluffy. Mix in pecans. Spread on cake.

CHRISTY'S FAVORITE CRUMB CAKE

This one is really hard to beat for flavor and for ease of preparation.

½ cup butter or margarine
1¼ cups sugar
2 eggs
1 cup plain yogurt
1 teaspoon vanilla
2 cups flour
1 teaspoon baking powder
½ teaspoon baking soda

4 tablespoons butter
2 tablespoons flour
½ cup brown sugar
1 teaspoon cinnamon
¼ cup chopped New Mexico pecans

Grease and flour a 9-inch square pan. Set oven at 350 degrees F. Cream butter and sugar well. Add eggs one at a time. Mix in yogurt and vanilla. Sift in dry ingredients and mix smooth. Turn into pan. Sprinkle topping over batter. Bake for 45 minutes. *Topping:* Work butter, flour, sugar, and cinnamon together until crumbly and mix in nuts.

GREEK SEMOLINA CAKE

This heavy, sticky, crunchy, and totally delicious cake comes from Albuquerque's Greek community and is quite different from anything you're likely to have made before.

3 cups semolina
1 cup sugar
1 cup milk
3 eggs
1 cup butter, melted
1 teaspoon cinnamon
¾ cup piñon nuts or pecans, roughly chopped

3 cups water
2 cups sugar
½ cup honey
1 teaspoon cinnamon
pecan halves

Set oven at 350 degrees F and grease an 8- or 9-inch square pan. Combine semolina, sugar, milk, eggs, butter, cinnamon, and nuts in a bowl and beat till well combined. Bake 40 to 45 minutes or until cooked through. Leave in pan to cool while you make this syrup: Combine water, sugar, honey, and cinnamon and boil hard for 15 minutes. Pour syrup over cake in pan and leave it for an hour or so until it is absorbed. Remove cake and decorate with pecan halves. Serve in thin wedges.

PUMPKIN LOAF

No book about New Mexican cooking would be complete without its share of pumpkin recipes. Here's a really easy loaf cake.

1 cup brown sugar
½ cup granulated sugar
1 cup mashed pumpkin (cooked or canned)
½ cup vegetable oil
2 eggs
2 cups flour
1 teaspoon bicarbonate of soda
½ teaspoon nutmeg
½ teaspoon cinnamon
¼ teaspoon ginger
1 cup raisins, chopped
½ cup chopped pecans
¼ cup water

Set oven at 350 degrees F and grease and flour a loaf pan. Put sugars, pumpkin, oil, and eggs in a bowl and beat well. Sift in flour, soda, nutmeg, cinnamon, and ginger and mix in. Add raisins, pecans, water, and mix well. Spoon into pan and bake 1¼-1½ hours or until done. Cool on wire rack. This will slice better the second day.

SANDY'S BROWN LOAF CAKE

You can eat your cake and have your health, too, with this recipe. Once more, we feature those New Mexico ingredients—pecans and honey.

1½ cups whole wheat flour
⅓ cup dry skim milk powder
½ cup wheat germ
2½ teaspoons baking powder
1 cup milk
½ cup honey
4 tablespoons oil
¾ cup chopped pecans

Set oven at 350 degrees F and grease a loaf pan. Combine flour, dry milk, wheat germ, and baking powder in a bowl. Pour in milk, honey, and oil, stir until just mixed. Fold in pecans. Bake 40-50 minutes. Cool on wire rack.

APRICOT GLAZE

Brush this over either the Pumpkin or the Brown Loaf Cakes.

¼ cup apricot jam, sieved or blended
1 teaspoon hot water

Mix and cook in a small saucepan until thin and syrupy. Brush over cake immediately.

BEST BROWNIES

These are absolutely the best brownies ever made, and one batch won't last 5 minutes around chocolate addicts.

½ cup butter or margarine
1 cup sugar
2 eggs
½ cup flour
1 cup chopped New Mexico pecans
2 squares unsweetened chocolate, melted
½ teaspoon vanilla
¼ teaspoon almond extract (optional)

Set oven at 350 degrees F and grease an 8-inch square pan. Cream butter, blend in sugar, and beat in eggs one at a time. Mix in flour. Stir in pecans and melted chocolate well, then mix in vanilla and almond extract. Bake 25-30 minutes. Don't overbake. Tops should be soft. Serve warm, cut in squares and topped with vanilla ice cream.

FRYING PAN COOKIES

Here's Rosalie Howland's favorite.

2 tablespoons butter
½ cup finely chopped dates
¾ cup raw sugar
2 eggs
½ cups chopped nuts
2 cups Special K cereal
1 teaspoon vanilla
shredded coconut

Melt butter, mix in dates, sugar, and eggs. Simmer for 8 minutes over low heat. Cool slightly. Add vanilla, cereal, and nuts. Mix well and form into balls. Roll in coconut.

PFEFFERNÜSSE

Sharlene and Klaus Wittern of Las Cruces celebrate a German Christmas. Klaus is an architect and developer who came from Germany in the 1960s. These spicy cookies—peppernuts—are traditional for Christmas.

3 eggs
¾ cup white sugar
¾ cup brown sugar
½ cup ground almonds
½ cup minced candied orange peel
¼ cup minced candied citron
2 teaspoons grated lemon rind
3 cups all-purpose flour
1 teaspoon cinnamon
¼ teaspoon ginger
¼ teaspoon fresh pepper
⅛ teaspoon ground cloves
¼ cup rum
confectioners' sugar

Beat eggs and sugars in large bowl until thick and lemon-colored. Stir in nuts, candied peels, and lemon rind. Sift flour, cinnamon, ginger, pepper and cloves into egg mixture. Stir until dough almost cleans side of bowl. Knead on lightly floured surface until smooth. Divide dough in half. Shape into 2 logs 1½ inches in diameter. Wrap in plastic and refrigerate 1 hour. Cut logs into ¾-inch slices. Place slices on greased baking sheets. Let stand uncovered at room temperature overnight. Heat oven to 325 degrees F. Turn cookies over and bake until centers are firm and tops are golden—15-20 minutes. Transfer to wire racks, brush generously with rum, sprinkle with sugar. Cool completely and age for 1-2 weeks. Makes 4 dozen.

CHOCOLATE NUT BARS

From a retired railroad man in Deming comes this cookie that makes good use of Las Cruces pecans. The base is crunchy and the top rich and gooey, a chocolate lover's joy.

1 cup flour
½ teaspoon baking powder
½ teaspoon bicarbonate of soda
1½ cups rolled oats
½ cup butter
½ cup sugar
2 tablespoons Karo syrup

6 ounces unsweetened chocolate
¼ cup butter or margarine
4 tablespoons Karo syrup
1 cup chopped pecans
½ cup flour
1 teaspoon vanilla

Heat oven to 350 degrees F. *Base:* Put flour, baking powder, soda, and oats in a bowl. Melt butter over low heat, stir in sugar and Karo, and cook until sugar dissolves. Stir into oat mixture. Press in bottom of greased 9-inch square pan and bake for 10 minutes. While it's baking, make the *Topping:* Melt chocolate, butter, and Karo together over low heat. When chocolate has melted, remove from heat and mix in pecans, flour, and vanilla. When base has baked 10 minutes, remove from oven and spread the chocolate mixture over it. Return to oven and bake 15 minutes longer or until the top is bubbling. Cool and cut into bars.

JAM SQUARES

oat pastry (see Chocolate Nut Bar recipe)
½ cup apricot or raspberry jam
½ cup sugar
1 egg
1 cup shredded coconut

Heat oven to 350 degrees F and grease a 9-inch square pan. Prepare oat pastry and press in bottom of pan. Bake for 10 minutes, then remove from oven. Cool 5 minutes. Sieve jam and spread on pastry. Beat sugar and egg together until light in color. Mix in coconut and spread over jam. Return to oven and bake 15-20 minutes more. Cut into squares.

PECAN MELTS

Here's another rich cookie from the pecan people at Stahmann Farms.

1 cup pecans
¾ cup sugar
2½ cups sifted flour
1 cup (½ pound) butter, softened

Put pecans through blender or processor and grind to a moist paste. Mix with remaining ingredients into a dough. (You could probably use whole wheat flour successfully with this recipe.) Roll into logs and chill until firm. Cut into ¼-inch slices and bake on ungreased cookie sheet for 15 minutes. Cool on wire rack. Dust with confectioners' sugar or decorate with dabs of simple white icing and bits of candied cherries.

PECAN-O COOKIES

This is the kind of nice basic nut cookie we all like to have in our repertoire.

½ cup margarine
½ cup granulated sugar
½ cup brown sugar
1 egg
¾ cup whole wheat flour
½ teaspoon cinnamon
¼ teaspoon nutmeg
1 cup rolled oats
½ cup chopped pecans
½ teaspoon vanilla

Cream margarine and sugars. Beat in egg. Mix in flour, cinnamon, and nutmeg well. Mix in oats, pecans and vanilla. Drop by teaspoonfuls on cookie sheets and bake at 350 degrees F for 10-12 minutes. Cool on wire racks.

PORTALES PEANUT COOKIES

It's hard to beat this classic—and healthful—recipe. Kids love these crisp cookies, and you will, too.

½ cup butter
½ cup crunchy peanut butter
1 cup brown sugar, firmly packed
1 egg
1 teaspoon vanilla
1 cup flour
¾ cup whole wheat flour
1 cup chopped Valencia peanuts

Cream the butter and peanut butter, then cream in brown sugar. Beat in the egg. Mix in vanilla, then stir in flours. The dough will be quite stiff. Roll into small balls, dip balls in chopped peanuts, and arrange on greased cookie sheet about an inch apart. With a fork, press each ball flat, first in one direction, then the other, so you have a tic-tac-toe pattern. (This seems to be traditional with peanut butter cookies!) Bake at 375 degrees F for 9-12 minutes, or until light brown.

GREEN TOMATO JAM

When the first frost warnings come over the radio in the fall, most home gardeners plunge outside to gather in the last of the tomatoes. But what do you do with a sack of big healthy tomatoes that didn't quite make it from green to red? Well, you can make green tomato pie, for one thing. (Just follow your favorite green apple pie recipe, using very thin slices of tomato instead of apple.) Or you can try this green tomato jam.

2 pounds green tomatoes
2 medium lemons
2 pounds sugar
2 ounces fresh ginger or 2 4-inch sticks cinnamon

Clean tomatoes and slice paper-thin. Slice lemons paper-thin, remove seeds, cover slices with water, and cook until skins are very tender. Measure the water that remains and add enough more to make 2 cups. Combine the water and sugar and cook to a thin syrup. Return lemons to syrup along with tomatoes and grated ginger or cinnamon sticks. Cook until tomatoes are clear and jam is thick—perhaps 1 hour. Remove cinnamon sticks if used and turn jam into sterilized jars.

GREEN TOMATO CHUTNEY

3½ pounds green tomatoes
½ pound green apples
½ pound yellow onions
1-2 fresh red chiles
1½ teaspoons minced fresh ginger root
1 cup brown sugar
1 teaspoon salt
1 cup seedless raisins
1½ cups cider vinegar

Chop up tomatoes; peel, core, and chop apples; peel and chop onions. Peel and seed chiles and chop. Put half the vinegar and all the remaining ingredients in a large heavy saucepan. Heat to boiling point, stirring constantly. Add remaining vinegar and simmer, stirring now and then, until mixture has become thick—about 1½ hours or longer. Seal in sterilized jars.

MORNING MUESLI

If you're dubious about the various sugars added to breakfast cereals, here's one you can make yourself. Serve cold with milk or make a hot cereal by adding boiling water.

½ pound unprocessed bran
1 pound rolled or quick-cooking oats
1 pound seedless raisins, chopped
1 pound dried apricots, chopped
½ cup shelled sunflower seeds
½ cup sesame seeds
1 cup wheat germ

Combine in a bowl, mix well, and store in an airtight container.

PEANUT BRITTLE

From Portales, the heart of the Valencia peanut country, comes an easy recipe.

2 cups sugar
1 cup chopped roasted peanuts
½ teaspoon salt

Butter a large pan or cookie sheet. In a heavy skillet, melt the sugar over low heat until it is a thin syrup. Stir constantly. Mix in nuts and salt. Pour in a thin sheet (you may have to tilt the baking sheet with your other hand, using a hot pot holder, of course). When candy is cold and hard, break into pieces.

APRICOT-PECAN BALLS

Glenna Rose Autrey makes these yummy all-natural candies that almost everyone adores.

¾ cup dried apricots
¾ cup flaked coconut
¾ cup chopped pecans
1 tablespoon lemon juice
½ teaspoon grated lemon rind
½ teaspoon grated orange rind
chopped nuts for coating

Wash and drain apricots. Add coconut and pecans. Put through a food grinder or processor. Add lemon juice and rinds. Knead with hands until blended. Roll into small balls, then roll in chopped nuts.

PIÑON CARAMELS

2 cups sugar
1¾ cups corn syrup
½ cup butter
2 cups evaporated milk
1 cup shelled piñon nuts
1 teaspoon vanilla

In a large heavy saucepan, combine sugar and corn syrup. Cook and stir over moderate heat to hard ball stage (245 degrees F on candy thermometer). Gradually stir in softened butter. Gradually add evaporated milk, slowly enough so mixture doesn't stop boiling. Continue cooking to firm ball stage again. Remove from heat. Stir in nuts and vanilla. Pour into buttered 9-inch square pan. Cool. Turn out and cut in squares. Wrap individually in plastic or waxed paper.

COFFEE PECAN FUDGE

Of course you'll want Las Cruces pecans for this!

3 cups sugar
1½ cups evaporated milk or cream
3 tablespoons corn syrup
2 tablespoons instant coffee granules
2 tablespoons butter
1 teaspoon vanilla
1 cup coarsely chopped pecans

Butter the sides of a large heavy saucepan. In it combine sugar, milk, corn syrup, and coffee. Heat to boiling, stirring constantly. Then boil to soft ball state (238 degrees F on candy thermometer). Remove from heat. Add butter, vanilla, and pecans, but don't stir. When fudge is lukewarm, beat until it begins to stiffen. Pour into buttered 9-inch square pan. Cool and cut in squares.

PECAN PRALINES

2 cups brown sugar
1 cup granulated sugar
1 cup cream
1 cup water
3 cups pecan halves

Heat sugars, cream, and water in a large heavy saucepan over low burner, stirring constantly, until sugars have dissolved. Increase heat and cook to soft ball stage (238 degrees F). Meanwhile, butter 2 large cookie sheets. Arrange clusters of 3 or 4 pecans on sheets. When candy is at soft ball stage, remove from heat and beat slightly with a wooden spoon. Then quickly, using a tablespoon, pour a spoonful of candy over each pecan cluster. When candies have cooled, store in an air-tight cannister. [For a more Mexican candy, try substituting shelled pumpkin seeds for the pecans. Stir seeds into the candy after you remove it from the heat. —SMC]

COLUMBUS QUINCE PASTE

This very Mexican sweet may also be made with guavas or mangoes. If you use either, skin and puree the fruit, then proceed as below.

8-10 quinces
4-5 cups sugar

Wash the quinces and steam or simmer for about 20-25 minutes or until tender. Cut in quarters and remove core and seeds. No need to peel. Puree in food processor or blender and measure. Add an equal amount of sugar. Put in a heavy pot and cook—and you must stir constantly!—until mixture is so thick that you can see the bottom of the pot clearly when you pull the wooden spoon through the paste. This will take about an hour. Cool, stirring occasionally. Put into small buttered molds or a flat pan lined with waxed paper. Unmold or cut in pieces to serve. Store in refrigerator or freezer. Serve as dessert or candy or with after-dinner cheeses.

RANCHO DE CHIMAYÓ COCKTAIL

This apple cocktail was created by Arturo Jaramillo, owner of the famous **Rancho de Chimayó** restaurant. A thoroughly New Mexican drink, it makes good use of Chimayó apples and cider.

1½ ounces tequila
1 ounce homemade New Mexico sweet apple cider
¼ ounce lemon juice
¼ ounce crème de cassis

Shake all ingredients together, chill, and serve with a wedge of New Mexico apple over the rim of the glass. Serves 1.

ROSALIE'S APRICOT BRANDY

Rosalie Howland says this is great to sip and is superb as a topping for vanilla ice cream.

1 pound dried apricots
1 pound sugar
1 quart vodka

Mix together in a glass container and store for 6 to 8 weeks in a cool dark place. Shake every other day or so, so flavors meld.

SEASONING SALT

Did you ever think of making your own special mix of seasoning salt? Rosalie Howland did, and uses this on baked potatoes, meat, popcorn, fish, eggs, and vegetables!

26 ounces salt (or sea salt)
1 ounce fresh ground black pepper
2 ounces ground red pepper
1 ounce pure garlic powder
1 ounce chile powder (especially Chimayó or Las Cruces)

Combine and mix. Put some in a shaker and store the rest in your pantry in a jar with a tight top.

SEASONING SALT II

Here's another version to consider.

1 cup salt
½ teaspoon white pepper
3 teaspoons Chimayó chile powder
½ teaspoon ground ginger
½ teaspoon cumin powder
1 teaspoon crushed dried oregano
½ teaspoon garlic powder
½ teaspoon onion powder

Combine and use.

We asked a number of well-known New Mexicans for their favorite foods and best recipes. Here we have their sometimes unusual responses.

BOILED WATER

Robin McKinney is the talented young publisher of the award-winning *Taos News*. When she's not busy at the office or pursuing her avocation of archaeology somewhere around the globe, Robin has started to learn to cook. She has generously given us this foolproof recipe—the one she says she's always sure she can do well.

Take one whole pot. Add water. Do not add too much water. A cup of water is enough for a cup of coffee. If you fill the pot to overflowing, boiling takes too long and uses too much fuel. A metal pot is best for boiling—porcelain ones tend to break on the stove. Remember to turn on the stove. When large bubbles start to rise from the bottom of the pot and break on the top of the water, the water is boiling. Use the water immediately. Do not let overflowing bathtubs, phone calls from irate subscribers, or anything else distract you, for if the pot boils dry, it may crack or melt. (A mild boiling-dry is not too serious: you can remove the sediment that forms in the bottom of the pot as a consequence of this by using cream of tartar. Cream of tartar is a powder—do not use tartar sauce, as it will stick to the sides of the pot and make future coffee and tea taste foul.) Then pour the boiling water out of the pot, being careful not to burn yourself with the steam, and there you are!

CARROT CAKE

Having mastered the basics, **Robin McKinney** has moved on to more complicated culinary delights, including this elegant cake.

2 cups sugar
2 cups flour
2 teaspoons baking powder
1 teaspoon cinnamon
½ teaspoon powdered cloves
½ teaspoon nutmeg
¼ teaspoon salt
4 eggs
1½ cups salad oil
1½ cups grated carrots
½ cup chopped New Mexico pecans

Grease and flour a bundt pan or angel cake pan, and preheat oven to 350 degrees F. Sift together the sugar, flour, baking powder, baking soda, cinnamon, cloves, nutmeg, and salt. In a separate bowl, mix together eggs and oil. Gradually add the dry ingredients, then when well blended add the grated carrots and chopped pecans. Bake for 50-60 minutes. Cool in pan on rack, then ease onto serving plate and serve plain or with cream cheese icing. (You could also dust it with confectioners' sugar or glaze it with a thin lemon glaze made of 2 teaspoons of lemon juice mixed with enough confectioners' sugar to make a thin icing.)

CREAM CHEESE ICING

1½ cups confectioners' sugar
3 ounces cream cheese
1 teaspoon vanilla

Blend well and spread thinly over the cooled cake.

ATOLE
(The Breakfast of Champions)

Rudolfo A. Anaya, the author of the novels *Bless Me Ultima, Heart of Aztlan,* and *Tortuga,* sends this healthy recipe from Santa Rosa.

Mix ½ cup of blue cornmeal into one cup of cold water. Mix thoroughly to dissolve the lumps. Pour into 1 cup of boiling water. Stir as you bring to a boil. Boil for 3 to 5 minutes, serve hot, as porridge, with honey and cream. Serves 2. Serve with buttered hot tortillas, bacon or sausage, juice, and marmalade. This is a low-calorie breakfast full of the spiritual goodness of the Southwest. My grandfather used to say, "A day without atole is like a day without sunshine."

The blue cornmeal may be bought anywhere in New Mexico, although some of the small ranches along the Río Grande Valley and the Indian pueblos have the best. Corn is not only one of the oldest cultivated plants of the New World, it has significance in the world of the sacred. A simple dish like atole puts one in touch with the New Mexican reality of earth and sky and growth and rain. That's why it is often called "the breakfast of champions." It has a wholesome goodness that outstrips the blander malt-o-meal or oatmeal. My grandfather lived to be 94, and he ate atole everyday. He was fond of spiking his with brandy, but I am not recommending that.

AVOCADO SOUP, LAS CRUCES

Maggie Gamboa of Las Cruces is a famous cook in southern New Mexico. Not only does she cater for parties, but she teaches cooking— including a chile gourmet class.

1 medium tomato
1 tablespoon minced onion
4 cups chicken broth
½ cup heavy cream
1 teaspoon lemon juice
2 large ripe avocados
¼ cup dry sherry
salt and pepper to taste
1 banana (optional)

Peel, seed, and chop the tomato. Place first 5 ingredients in blender or processor and blend well. Heat this mixture in a saucepan and simmer for a few minutes. Peel and mash avocados and stir into soup. Add sherry, salt and pepper to taste, and heat well, but do not allow to boil. Serve hot or cold. Decorate each bowl with two or three thin slices of banana for an extra touch of flavor. Serves 6.

FIESTA DIP

Maggie Gamboa has been more than generous in sharing some of her special party recipes.

1 8-ounce package of cream cheese
½ cup hot or mild taco sauce
1 4-ounce can chopped green chile
2 tablespoons minced onion
½ teaspoon cumin powder
¼ teaspoon salt

Mix together in a large bowl until well blended. Makes about 1½ cups. Serve with corn chips or tostadas.

NOPALITOS

Maggie Gamboa has so many unusual recipes that it's hard to decide which ones to use. But, as most of us are familiar with the sight of prickly pears but have no idea how to use them as food, perhaps Maggie's help is most important in this area. Here's what she has to say on the subject:

The nopal, or prickly pear cactus, is no stranger to the people of the Southwest. It grows in most desert areas, and the fruit of the prickly pear is used as a vegetable or made into syrups, jams, jellies, and candy.

It is important to know about the nopal because it could save your life if you were ever lost in the desert. The nopal is used extensively in Mexico and tastes somewhat like string beans. It can be purchased in many supermarkets, either fresh or prepared in jars.

You might want to plant one in your garden. Just plant one joint of a prickly pear cactus. As it grows, remove the young pads, clean and cook them. They are very good in chile or an omelet.

To clean: Hold the pad with a fork to avoid getting thorns in your fingers, then with a very sharp knife cut off the thorns. Then peel or scrape a very thin layer from the pad. DO NOT PEEL TOO MUCH.

Take 4 young cactus pads, slice in 1-inch strips and rinse in cold water. Put in saucepan and cover with cold water. Add 1 tablespoon salt and 1 tablespoon bicarbonate of soda, and simmer for 25 minutes. (The soda cuts the sticky juice, which is quite a bit like the juice of cooked okra. This trick works for okra, too.) After 25 minutes, check for tenderness. Remove from heat, drain, and rinse with cold water. Pat dry with paper towels. Serve heated in chile sauce, or one of the following ways.

NOPALITOS WITH EGGS

1 cup prepared nopalitos (see above)
1 small onion, minced
3 tablespoons oil
3 green chiles, chopped
1 fresh tomato, chopped
3 eggs, beaten
salt and pepper to taste

Heat oil in skillet and saute onion until translucent. Mix in chiles, tomato, cactus, and then eggs. Mix well and add salt and pepper. Turn off heat as soon as eggs are set. Serve for breakfast with ham or bacon. Serves 2-3.

CACTUS WITH PORK

2 cups prepared nopalitos
1 cup cubed cooked pork
2 tablespoons oil
1 medium onion, chopped
1/3 cup chopped tomatoes (cooked or canned)
pinch of oregano
salt and pepper to taste

Fry the pork in oil. Add onion and saute until translucent. Drain off excess fat. Mix in remaining ingredients and simmer for about 10 minutes.

FRANK WATERS'S LENTIL SOUP

Like many another writer, **Frank Waters,** the Taos patriarch of Southwestern authors, appreciates the simple things of life. This hearty lentil soup is a particular favorite, one which he often prepares for guests. Barbara Waters admits that when she ventured to suggest to one haughty old Russian aristocrat that it might have a "Russian" flavor, he informed them, "We feed this to our *pigs!*" Those pigs of bygone years must have eaten well indeed! Frank believes "A good cook should play it by ear," and he adjusts the seasonings to taste.

If you have had a baked ham, you might use the bone and leftover bits of meat instead of the ham hocks. A great meal, this, for a cold winter's evening by the fire.

12 ounces lentils
1 large onion, chopped
1 cup celery, including tops, chopped
4-6 sprigs parsley, chopped
1 bay leaf
½ teaspoon thyme
½ teaspoon basil
¼ teaspoon rosemary
¼ teaspoon garlic salt
2 ham hocks
salt and pepper to taste

Pick over lentils and soak for 3 hours in cold water. Drain, rinse and cover with approximately 3½ quarts of water. Add remaining ingredients except ham hocks, salt and pepper. Simmer for an hour. Add the ham hocks and simmer for another 2 hours (longer if you live at a high altitude). Add more water if necessary to maintain at least the 3-quart mark. Remove ham hocks from soup. Eliminate skin and fat, and cut meat into bite-size pieces. Put bones and meat back into soup. Season to taste with salt and pepper. Simmer 20-30 minutes longer. Serve with tossed salad and French rolls or Indian bread.

SUNSHINE GAZPACHO

In New Mexico publishing circles, **R. Guy Hankins** is well known as the president and publisher of the award-winning *Las Cruces Sun-News*. But among playwrights and would-be actors, he may be better known as one of the charter members of Corporate Support of the Arts, an organization that has put the New Mexico State University drama department on the United States map with its funding of their innovative programs. Guy recommends this marvelous cold soup that originated in Spain to be served "on our beautiful warm New Mexico days."

1 small clove fresh garlic
4 cups chicken broth
½ medium bell pepper
2 large ripe tomatoes
½ medium cucumber
½ medium onion
½ ripe avocado
2 small tender stalks of celery
2 tablespoons fresh lemon juice
salt and pepper to taste

Press the peeled garlic into the chicken broth. Remove seeds and veins from bell pepper. Peel tomatoes and cucumber. Finely chop all vegetables and stir with lemon juice and seasonings into broth. Cover and refrigerate until well chilled. (This allows flavors to meld.) Guy notes that one nice thing about this soup is that you may add more or less of any of the vegetables, or add others to suit your taste. Crusty garlic or cheese bread would make a happy accompaniment to this delectable soup.

SPARKLING GAZPACHO

Mark Medoff is artistic director in the Department of Theatre Arts at New Mexico State University in Las Cruces. More important, his play, *Children of a Lesser God*, won a Tony Award, the Outer Critics Circle and Drama Desk awards for the best Broadway play of 1980, and *When You Comin' Back, Red Ryder?* won an Obie, and the Critics Circle and Drama Desk awards in 1973. He enjoys this version of gazpacho.

1 12-ounce can tomato juice (1½ cups)
4 medium-sized tomatoes
2 medium-sized cucumbers
¼ cup chopped green pepper
¼ cup sliced green onion
1 small clove garlic, minced or mashed
3 tablespoons olive oil
3 tablespoons wine vinegar
½ teaspoon chile powder
½ teaspoon liquid hot pepper seasoning
dash, ground cloves
1 10-ounce bottle club soda
finely diced jalapeño pepper (optional)

Pour tomato juice into a large bowl. Peel tomatoes and dice, discarding most of the seedy portions. Peel and dice cucumber. Add to the bowl the tomato, cucumber, green pepper, green onion, garlic, olive oil, vinegar, chile powder, liquid hot pepper, and cloves. For chunky consistency, do not puree, simply dice the vegetables. Mix well, cover and refrigerate until well chilled, at least 4 hours or overnight. Stir again just before serving and stir in the club soda. Ladle into chilled bowls. Those who enjoy true heat may add diced jalapeño peppers at serving. Serves 6 to 8.

POTATO SOUP HILLERMAN

As the creator of those redoubtable Navajo detectives, Joe Leaphorn and Jim Chee, **Tony Hillerman** is becoming as well known to mystery fans as Arthur Upfield or Dick Francis. But never mind serving exotic dishes to Tony, whose latest book is *The Dark Wind*. "I am a life-long soup lover," he says, "and this is my favorite."

4 cups diced raw potatoes
½ cup diced onion
½ cup diced celery
2 cups cream or half-and-half
2 tablespoons butter
salt and pepper to taste
chopped parsley or chives

In a heavy pot place potatoes, onion and celery, and add enough water to barely cover. Cook, covered, until tender but not mushy. Stir in the cream and butter, and add salt and pepper to taste. Heat to boiling, but do not allow to boil. Remove from heat and serve sprinkled with parsley or chives.

JIM CHEE'S SOPAIPILLAS

It's a fact of life that sopaipillas, New Mexico's tender, crispy fat puffs of bread, always seem to cook better at high altitudes and taste better when eaten in crystalline mountain air. Nevertheless, they still taste fantastic and evoke fond memories, even when eaten in tropic jungles. This is one way of making them. Another is with yeast— and you might try Fern Lyon's magic dough recipe on page 19.

2 cups flour
2 teaspoons baking powder
1 teaspoon salt
2 tablespoons lard
½ cup water
oil or lard for deep frying

Sift dry ingredients together. Work in lard, then lukewarm water, to make a soft dough. Chill in refrigerator. Roll out dough on floured surface to about 1/4 inch. Cut into 3-inch squares. Drop into hot lard (400 degrees F) a few at a time. Brown on each side and drain on paper towels. Serve hot. To eat, nip off a corner and pour in honey.

CAPONATA

Marianna Gabbi is conductor and musical director of the Las Cruces Symphony Orchestra and a member of the music faculty of New Mexico State University. Besides all that, she's an expert cook. She won first prize in a contest with this recipe, which she says is extremely versatile—like the lady herself. It can be served hot or cold as an appetizer, salad, vegetable, or even crêpe filling.

1 large eggplant
4 medium bell peppers
3 very ripe tomatoes
2 medium onions
¼ cup olive oil
¼ teaspoon sugar
salt and pepper
½ cup white vinegar
1 cup water
pitted green olives (optional)

Wash, dry and peel eggplant, and dice into 1-inch squares. Dice peppers, peel tomatoes. Slice onions thinly. Saute peppers in olive oil until tender. Remove, and saute onions until golden in same oil. Add eggplant and saute for 10 minutes. Cut up tomatoes and add to the mixture, and cook for 5 minutes. Mix in sauteed peppers, vinegar, sugar, salt and pepper, and 1 cup water. Simmer over medium heat for about 30 minutes, or until water evaporates. Mix in pitted green olives if desired. Mixture can be refrigerated for a week.

CHILE COLORADO CON CARNE

Rubén González, who lives in Bayard in southern New Mexico, is noted for his construction paintings and metal sculpture. Rubén's interest in metal came about naturally—he and his father were both copper miners in the rich mines near Silver City. Rubén says this favorite recipe has real Mexican flavor.

3 pounds round steak
3 tablespoons cooking oil
3 10-ounce cans red enchilada sauce, mild or hot
1 medium onion
1 teaspoon salt
¼ teaspoon marjoram
¼ teaspoon oregano
¼ teaspoon cinnamon
¼ teaspoon sugar
1 tablespoon Gebhardt's chile powder
1 tablespoon Worcestershire sauce

Cut steak into 3/4-inch cubes. In a large heavy pan, brown the steak *well* in cooking oil. Chop the onion—there should be about ½ cup—and add to the meat. When onion has become transparent, gradually stir in the enchilada sauce. (Rubén uses Las Palmas or Mountain Pass brands.) Add remaining ingredients, and stir well. Cover and simmer slowly for about 30 minutes. Serves 8.

Rubén says that 3 pounds of cooked roast beef may be used instead of the round steak. And he stresses that it is most important to use the chile powder, cinnamon, and sugar in order to give the dish the traditional flavor.

ROSA DE NARANJA DE MOSQUERO

Morris Rippel is a well-known painter of New Mexico scenes. A former architect, he designed the Albuquerque house he and his wife Betsy live in. This favorite dish, an elegant spinoff of the taco, was invented by Betsy.

1 quart homemade red chile sauce (see page 8)
1 cup fresh chopped green chile (see page 7)
1 pound lean ground round
12 corn tortillas, preferably blue corn
vegetable oil
salt and pepper to taste
½ pound jack cheese, grated
½ pound cheddar cheese, grated
4 green onions, minced
2 large tomatoes, cut in 8 wedges
chopped lettuce
ripe olives, sliced
2 large oranges, peeled, cut in 5 slices, then quartered
piñon nuts
1 cup water

Prepare chile sauce and green chile. Fry ground round in a tablespoon of oil in heavy skillet until meat is well done and lightly browned. Stir in 1 cup chile sauce and 1 cup water. Add salt and pepper to taste. Let simmer until all moisture has absorbed. Fry tortillas in vegetable oil until pliable but not crisp. Drain on paper towels. Mix cheeses together. Heat red chile sauce. To assemble: Place tortilla on oven-proof plate, add 1 tablespoon meat mixture, green chile, grated cheese. Fold over. When desired number of tortillas have been assembled on each plate, cover with red chile sauce, and sprinkle with green onions and cheese. Bake at 400 degrees F until sauce bubbles. Arrange lettuce, tomato wedges and orange "roses" on plate. Sprinkle a strip of sliced olives and piñon nuts across top. Serve to 4 with ice cold beer by candlelight.

CHICKEN TERIYAKI WITH SESAME

The popular and talented conductor of the New Mexico Symphony Orchestra, **Yoshimi Takeda,** is a well-known gourmet cook who specializes in Oriental cooking.

1 pound boned chicken, breast or thigh
6 tablespoons soy sauce
6 tablespoons sake or white wine
6 tablespoons sesame oil
1 clove garlic, crushed
2 teaspoons minced ginger root
1 tablespoon sugar
6 tablespoons pan-toasted sesame seeds

Cut chicken into bite-size pieces. Combine remaining ingredients except sesame seeds. Marinate chicken in this mixture for at least an hour, turning once or twice. Drain and skewer chicken on bamboo picks. Broil for 5 or 6 minutes, turning once. Roll in sesame seeds and serve hot. Serves 4-6.

GREEN RICE

2 cups watercress, finely chopped
2 tablespoons white vinegar
2-3 tablespoons black or light sesame seeds
¼ teaspoon salt
4 cups hot cooked long-grain rice
green and red grape clusters
watercress sprigs

In a medium saucepan cook watercress, uncovered, in small amount of boiling salted water for 2 minutes. Drain well, pressing out excess moisture between paper towels. Stir together vinegar, sesame seeds and salt; toss with rice and watercress. Spoon mixture onto a serving platter. Garnish with grape clusters and sprigs of watercress. Makes 8 servings.

CHICKEN ENCHILADA PIE FITZPATRICK

George Fitzpatrick, who was for 35 years the beloved editor of **New Mexico Magazine,** says this is his favorite dinner—"I really get hungry for it," he says. George's grandson became so addicted to the dish that at 17 he got the recipe and began making it for himself and anyone else in California who wanted it. George isn't the only one who craves this—several people told us it's their favorite recipe and submitted variations on the theme. Not only is it good, but it's easy.

1½ cups cubed cooked chicken
¼ cup butter
1 medium onion, chopped
1 can cream of chicken soup
1 4-ounce can chopped green chiles
10 ounces sharp cheddar cheese, grated
1 medium bag taco-flavored tortilla chips

Saute the onion in the butter in a large skillet. When onion is clear, add the chicken, soup,· ¾ soup can of water, and green chiles. Mix and simmer for 30 minutes. In an 8 x 8 x 2 baking dish spread a layer of half the tortilla chips. Spread with half the sauce, then sprinkle with half the grated cheese. Layer with the remaining chips, the remaining sauce, and the remaining cheese. Bake for 30 minutes at 350 degrees F. Serves 6-8.

CHICKEN DIVAN

Bill Mauldin's cartoons have been winning prizes and worldwide acclaim ever since he left his native New Mexico to draw the soldiers Willie and Joe during World War II. He is now with the *Chicago Sun-Times*, and his cartoons are syndicated.

6 chicken breast halves
1 medium onion, halved
3 celery stalks, whole or halved
2-3 carrots, whole
½ unpeeled lemon
salt and pepper to taste

1 bunch fresh broccoli spears
    (or 2 10-ounce packages frozen
    broccoli spears). Leave whole.
2 10½-ounce cans cream of chicken soup
1 cup mayonnaise
¼-½ cup sherry (to taste)

½-¾ cup parmesan cheese
1 cup bread crumbs, maybe more

Boil chicken breasts with onion, celery, carrots, lemon half and salt and pepper to taste in water to cover for about 2 hours. Take out chicken, which will be falling off the bones, and remove skin and bones. (Keep broth and vegetables for soup or other future use.) While chicken is cooking, cook broccoli separately. Make a sauce by mixing the chicken soup, mayonnaise, and sherry.

Grease a large *flat* baking dish (13½ x 8 ¾ x 1 ¾ would be fine) and layer all the broccoli spears on the bottom. Pour on half of the sauce. Arrange the chicken in more or less bite-size pieces over the broccoli layer, and add the rest of the sauce. Cover the top well with parmesan cheese and finish off with a generous layer of bread crumbs. Bake at 350 degrees F for 30 minutes. Serves 4-6.

RALSTON HASH

Shakespeare, New Mexico's most famous ghost town and one of the most intact, is owned by **Rita and Janaloo Hill,** mother and daughter. About two miles south of Lordsburg, it is open for tours the second Sunday of each month from 10 a.m. to 2 p.m. Rita and Janaloo suggest this modern version of a dish that in times gone by would have been made with chicos (dried sweet corn) and dried chile. Shakespeare was known as Ralston City from 1870 to 1879.

1½ pounds ground meat (venison, antelope, or beef)
2 16-ounce cans cream-style corn
1 3-ounce can chopped green chile
1 tablespoon sugar
salt to taste

Fry ground meat in a large skillet, stirring until it is well done and lightly browned. Drain off any excess grease. Stir in corn, chile, sugar and salt. Bring to boil and simmer for 5 minutes, stirring regularly. Serve with frijoles. Serves 6.

BEEF TACOS ROMERO

Rubén Romero is a leading classical guitarist. He plays flamenco, Bach, Albéniz and his own compositions—as well as a variety of other music for classical guitar. He has appeared as soloist with the Denver and New Mexico symphony orchestras. Most of these ingredients can be kept on hand for an impromptu party.

1 pound ground round
2 tablespoons vegetable oil
1 large onion, minced
1 package taco seasoning (Casados Farms preferred)
8 taco shells
1 pound cheddar cheese, grated
1 large tomato, sliced
1 head lettuce shredded
1 bottle salsa picante, medium hot

Fry meat in oil in heavy skillet, stirring so it is well broken up. Mix in 1 tablespoon of the minced onion, then stir in taco seasoning. Meanwhile, put taco shells in 350-degree F oven to warm. Do not brown them. Drain excess fat from meat and put a good couple spoonfuls in each shell. Then add to your liking the raw onion, tomato, lettuce, and cheese. Splash on salsa picante to your taste. Serves 4 with 2 tacos each—or 2 persons with 4 tacos each.

RED BEANS AND RICE

Richard Bradford, author of *Red Sky at Morning* and *So Far From Heaven,* is a noted gourmet as well as a noted author. Richard, like many another avid New Mexican, came from "somewhere else"— in his case, New Orleans. He says, "This is the quintessential New Orleans dish, as beloved and familiar to Orleanians as warm rain, the Mississippi River, or a mother's lullaby. It is also the perfect medicine for those unfortunates who suffer from carbohydrate starvation."

1 pound dried red kidney beans
2 ham hocks (or ham bone with some meat on it)
1 cup chopped green onions
1 medium onion, chopped
1 clove garlic, minced
4 tablespoons butter
1 teaspoon dried thyme
salt and pepper to taste
2 cups uncooked long-grain rice

Wash the beans and soak overnight in 6 cups water. Next day drain the beans, reserving the soaking water. Add enough more fresh water to make 6 cups. Set aside beans and liquid. In a large heavy pot, melt butter and stir in onion, garlic, and *half* the green onions. Saute until soft and transparent. Stir in beans and liquid, pepper and thyme. Add ham hocks, preferably sawed in 2 or 3 pieces. Bring to boil, then simmer, partially covered, until beans are soft—1 to 4 hours. If beans get too dry, add a little hot water from time to time. When beans are tender, take a large spoon and mash some against the side of the pot to thicken the liquid. Remove ham bones, cut off meat, dice it and return to pot. Discard bones and fat. Add salt to taste. Cook rice until it is fluffy. Serve beans and rice in separate bowls. Serve yourself (in deep soup bowls) with beans spooned over the rice. Garnish with remaining chopped green onions. Other possible additions to set on the table as condiments in New Orleans might include wine vinegar, vinaigrette poured off the salad, or such pepper sauces as Trappey's or Tabasco. Serves 6.

ZUCCHINI PIE

William Kirschke is the artistic director and conductor of the Orchestra of Santa Fe. What makes this pie special, he says, is the dynamic taste it derives from the mustard.

3 eggs
4 cups sliced zucchini
1 cup diced onion
1 teaspoon basil
1 teaspoon thyme
½ teaspoon oregano
2 tablespoons butter
2 cups grated jack or cheddar cheese
2 tablespoons dijon mustard
1 9-inch unbaked pie shell

Preheat oven to 375 degress F. Saute zucchini, onion, and herbs in butter. Beat eggs in a large bowl. Stir in cheese and then zucchini mixture. Spread mustard over bottom of pie shell. Pour in zucchini filling. Bake for 30-40 minutes or until knife inserted near center comes out clean. Serves 4-6.

CHILES RELLENOS IN TEMPURA BATTER

To say that **Roy Nakayama** is a professor in the Department of Horticulture at New Mexico State University's College of Agriculture and Home Economics is to understate the story. For Roy is the foremost chile expert of the United States—and probably the world. He has developed new varieties, upgraded and standardized older varieties, improved chile farmers' crops—and devised the famous Nakayama scale of chile hotness (see *The Best From New Mexico Kitchens*). It's not surprising, then, that Roy suggests chiles rellenos as one of his favorite recipes. But this one has a difference—Japanese tempura batter.

½ cup flour
½ cup cornstarch
1 teaspoon baking powder
¼ teaspoon MSG
1 egg
2/3 cup water

8-10 green chiles, peeled and seeded
½ pound cheese (longhorn, cheddar or jack)
vegetable oil

Mix flour, cornstarch, baking powder, and MSG in a bowl. Beat egg and water together with a fork, then stir into dry mixture. Let thick batter stand for 30 minutes or longer before using. Add more water if thinner batter is desired. DO NOT MIX TOO VIGOROUSLY. Use whole, peeled fresh chiles or canned whole green chiles. Make small opening in pods and carefully insert a piece of cheese approximately an inch wide, ¼ inch thick, and 4 inches long. Blot off excess surface water with dry paper towel and place the prepared pod in batter. Heat about ¾ inch oil in heavy skillet to 360 degrees F. Cook batter-coated pods until golden brown. Remove and drain off excess oil. Serves 3-4.

QUESADILLAS DE MAPIMI

Michael Hurd is the son of the famous and popular painters, Peter Hurd and Henriette Wyeth. Also an artist, Michael is painting his own name into the annals of this talented family. He lives on the family ranch at San Patricio. About his cooking, Michael says, "I gratefully acknowledge the advice and gentle warnings of several great cooks, including Oliva Miranda, Annie Peña, Alfredo Martínez, and Vernon Taylor III. I also recommend Mesilla Valley chile from the farm of Refugio Montoya in La Mesa, New Mexico!"

2 cups masa harina flour
1½ cups rain water
⅛ teaspoon salt
bacon grease or Crisco
menonitas cheese
oregano
garlic powder
green chiles, peeled and cut in strips

Michael says good tortillas are "flat necessary" for this recipe, so it is imperative you make your own from scratch. Stir rain water into the masa harina and salt. Mix well, knead, and shape into thin tortillas. (Use your hands or a tortilla press.) Slap tortillas onto hot *comal* or grill, which has been greased with bacon fat or Crisco. Brown on one side, then turn tortilla over, adding thin slices of Mexican menonitas cheese, which should melt nicely. Sprinkle lightly with oregano and garlic powder, add strips of green chile, and fold tortilla in half. Serve piping hot with plenty of cold Mexican beer.

MEXIWEGIAN SANDWICH

E. A. Mares is one of the leading poets of New Mexico. His work appears in the anthologies *The Indian Río Grande, Southwest, Festival de Floricanto*, and *Ceremony of Brotherhood*. He is also a freelance writer. Sometimes he is a professor. Tony claims he really can't cook, but that is belied by this recipe, which he made up—including this introduction:

Rumor has it that long ago two lost exploration parties, one Norwegian and the other Mexican, met somewhere on the North American continent. Within days they parted and continued their voyages, but somehow they had enough time together to create an unforgettable sandwich, the renowned "Mexiwegian." Although the recipe has undergone changes over the centuries, oral tradition has kept the essentials intact and handed them down to a small but knowledgeable group of connoisseurs. The sandwich is sometimes called "Explorers Delight," or the "Long Distance Sandwich." This latter term refers to its high protein content that dispels hunger for many hours. It does not refer, as its detractors claim, to "the long distance to the grave" that it will take you or to "the long distance your friends will keep from you" after you have enjoyed this delicacy.

2 corn or wheat tortillas or slices whole wheat bread
1 clove garlic, minced
2 tablespoons fresh chopped chile (canned will do)
3 tablespoons soft goat cheese (or cottage cheese)
2 slices Swiss cheese
1 tin Norwegian sardines (fresh or dried sardines preferred)
3 whole green chiles (optional)

Heat tortillas if using. Mix goat cheese (or cottage cheese), garlic and chopped chile, and spread on one tortilla. Add slices of Swiss cheese. Next put on a layer of 3 or 4 small brisling sardines. For extra taste and flavor, add whole fresh green chiles. Finally, add the second tortilla or bread slice, pressing it down firmly. You now have a Mexiwegian. Tony adds: "Almost any beverage goes well with the Mexiwegian."

SOURDOUGH BREAD

John L. Sinclair is a cowboy who really lived those enchanted days of yesteryear—and wrote about them. He has written for **New Mexico Magazine** since 1937. His novels include In *Time of Harvest, Death in the Claim Shack,* and *Cousin Drewey and the Holy Twister.* Among his nonfiction titles are *New Mexico: The Shining Land* and *Cowboy Riding Country.* Here's his recipe for sourdough bread as he got it from Bill Kelsey, these many years ago:

Bread for the cowboy of 50 years ago never came in loaf form, nor was its dough made of any other flour but the white bleached variety. Loaf bread was contemptuously called "gun waddin', " and whole wheat was something to be fed to the chickens. The pride of the saddleman was that gem of the dutch oven called sourdough, the biscuit with a character all its own.

Bill Kelsey, who lived against the hills of Lincoln County's Hondo Valley way back from the early day, and whom I knew and worked for at intervals in the late 1920s and early '30s, was a slim and rugged combination of cowboy, teamster, chuck-wagon cook, dry land or irrigation farmer and master craftsman of the building of wolf-proof fences over the roughest terrain imaginable—netting and barbed wire guaranteed to keep coyotes out.

Examples still stretch mile upon mile across the rocky zacahuista hills as a memorial to his genius. Old Bill worked on well into his 90s. He was found dead beside a freshly dug hole, a cedar post held in his lifeless arms—he'd been in the process of building a new fence around his home.

Out in camp, Bill displayed another talent born to the frontiersman, the knack of satisfying a crew of fence builders all packing fresh-air appetites. He served up the most delectable of rangeland food cooked under potrack and over hardwood coals—bacon and beans, fried potatoes, stewed dried fruits, rice and raisins, coffee black as tar and, glory be, dutch oven sourdough bread.

Fill an earthen crock half-full of flour and water, half and half. Add a yeast cake [or dry yeast—SMC], tie a cloth over the top to form a cover, and let it sour in a warm place for 2 or 3 days. Then put 2 or 3 tablespoons of lard in a cow-camp dutch oven, the kind with the raised rim around the lid, and lay it and the lid separately in the hot coals under the potrack, so as to heat them and melt the lard. Mix in a pan (Bill never used measurements) flour, salt, baking soda, baking powder, and sugar—the last to give the biscuits a brown crust—and lard to be hand-worked into the dry mixture. [We'll have to guess, too. How about 2 cups of flour, maybe ½ teaspoon of baking soda, 1 of baking powder, 2 tablespoons of sugar and ¼ cup lard?—SMC.] Make a depression in the center and pour in enough sourdough mixture to make the number of biscuits the dutch oven will hold. [Try 1 cup or so—SMC.] Work into a dough as you would ordinary baking powder biscuits. Roundup cooks never used a biscuit cutter but artfully managed to shape them with their hands. Dredge the beauties in the hot lard in the oven. Arrange them together as in any baking pan.

Take a shovelful of hot coals from the fire. Always use hardwoods such as oak or walnut if you want long-lasting coals. Spread coals on the ground, about the diameter of the oven. On this place the oven. Cover with the hot lid, and on this spread another shovelful of hot coals. Take a rest, drink coffee, and wait. If there's anyone around, shoot windies with him—tell bigger lies than he can. Camp cooks know how long it takes. You'll learn. [Maybe you should have a look after 15 or 20 minutes?—SMC.] But in time you'll use a pothook to lift the lid—and there, delightful to your eyes and delicious to your nose, will be a mess of brown-topped sourdough biscuits, ready to pop into your mouth. You will always have sourdough in the crock if you add the same quantity of flour and water that you took out. The crock should be "fed" every week. [There are stories in the West of cherished sourdough mixtures that started in the 1700s—or earlier—and are still going. . .strong.—SMC.]

LEMON ANGEL PIE

Gordon Snidow has been called the Rembrandt of the Range, and little wonder. His paintings of today's cowboys and ranchers are alive with the emotion of the moment, and the dramatic play of light and shadow, the textures of leather, wood, and wrinkled skin recall masterpieces of the past. Meanwhile, back home on the range in Ruidoso, Gordon's choice of food is not the heavy fare you might expect. This light and lemony torte is his absolute all-time favorite dessert.

4 egg whites
½ teaspoon cream of tartar
1 cup sugar

4 egg yolks
½ cup sugar
4 tablespoons lemon juice
grated rind of 1 lemon
1 cup heavy cream, whipped

Beat egg whites frothy. Add cream of tartar and beat stiff. As eggs stiffen, add 2 tablespoons of sugar at a time until you have added the full cup. Pile into an ungreased pie tin with high sides, shaping the meringue to be higher on the sides. Bake 40 minutes at 300 degrees F. Cool. Meanwhile, beat egg yolks thick, add sugar, lemon juice and rind. Cook, stirring constantly, in the top of a double boiler over hot, not boiling, water until mixture is thick and spongy. Cool. Fold in whipped cream and turn into baked meringue shell. Refrigerate until serving time.

DATE BARS

As a singer, composer, and recording artist, **David Salazar** is possibly even more popular in Mexico than in New Mexico and the southwestern United States. David, a native of Española, says this is his favorite dessert.

¼ **cup melted butter**
½ **cup molasses**
3 eggs, beaten well
1 cup whole wheat flour
½ **teaspoon baking powder**
⅛ **teaspoon salt**
1 cup chopped pitted dates
1 cup chopped nuts (any kind)

Mix all ingredients together and spread in a 14 x 8 buttered pan. Bake at 350 degrees F for approximately 30 minutes, or until light brown. Don't overbake. Cut in squares and serve warm topped with a scoop of coffee ice cream.

MARGUERITES

Mary Elizabeth King is the director of the highly esteemed University Museum at New Mexico State University. Liz got this very unusual recipe from her grandmother.

3 egg whites
1 pound super-fine granulated sugar, sifted
½ pound seedless raisins
½ pound walnut meats, chopped
1 box saltines

Beat egg whites stiff. Fold in sugar, raisins and nuts. (Hint: If you don't have extra-fine sugar, run ordinary granulated sugar in food processor for a minute or two, and you'll have it.) Spread mixture on unsalted side of crackers. Bake at 350 degrees F until lightly browned. Cool on cookie racks.

FRUIT PEMMICAN

Ruth Armstrong is an Albuquerque-based travel writer whose features—often about New Mexico—appear in newspapers and magazines all over the country. She's also an outdoors addict.

1 package each: dried apples, apricots, peaches, prunes
1 cup chopped nuts
½ cup butter or margarine
½ cup honey
½ cup peanut butter
½ cup instant coffee (optional)
toasted wheat germ

Grind or process the apples, apricots, peaches, and prunes, or any other combination you prefer. Mix in remaining ingredients well. You'll have to use your hands. Shape into fat fingers or bars, and roll each piece in toasted wheat germ. Wrap in waxed paper, put in plastic bag and freeze. Take out as needed.

Where to find your New Mexico cooking supplies when you live far from any local sources is often a problem. Although most large supermarkets and gourmet delicatessens carry canned and frozen items like tortillas, chiles and sauces, few stock blue cornmeal, for example. And residents in small remote towns may have difficulty finding chiles at all. The following sources are able to help, and they handle mail orders. In addition, check advertisements in **New Mexico Magazine** for new sources. Write or call to find out about products and prices before sending any money.

Los Chileros de nuevo mexico, inc.
1201 Cerrillos Road, Suite 7
Santa Fe, New Mexico 87501
(505) 982-6294

Orlando A. Casados
P.O. Box 1149
San Juan Pueblo, NM 87566
(505) 852-4356

Las Cruces Foods, Inc.
P.O. Box 98
Mesilla Park, NM 88047
(505) 526-2352

Index

Index

Index